LET THE JOURNEY
BEGIN

Acknowledgements

This book is for my daughter, Sarina, who first introduced me to TikTok and put up with me during the past year as I went on this unknown journey.

Thanks to my parents, Shirin and Ali; first, for bringing me into this world and for going through the hardship of moving to Canada from Iran when I was a teenager so we could have a better future. Thanks to my old friends, who have always been there for me through ups and downs and the new friends I met virtually (special thanks to the OG group- Becca, Gabe, Nick, Peter, and Dave) who supported my TikTok journey. Thanks to my brothers, who encouraged me to create a journal and a book out of all the questions I asked over the past year.

Thank you for reading this book and trusting me to guide you through your journey by sharing what thousands of others shared. This book will be a tool to help you think outside the box and start finding your path, whatever it might be.

How this all began

The world has been upside down for most of us since the pandemic started, and many people have suffered from being isolated. I posted my first video on TikTok on Dec 20, 2021, introducing myself to spread positive vibes and create more awareness about well-being, not knowing what to expect.

I started posting videos daily and hosting ongoing live conversations, and soon my page became that "safe space" for people to come together and share their stories and struggles. The need to be heard, loved, and accepted echoed strongly with people, especially during the pandemic. As I was connecting with this new community, I learned to truly listen when someone says, "I am fine," because what they are trying to say, what they genuinely need you to hear, is, "Please help me!" These three small words packed in so much power, used as a two-way shield, protecting us from the world and them from us.

Having spent a lengthy career in healthcare, I knew most people are not proactive about their well-being until something is broken. Even then, they don't know all their options, which is precisely why I created a health app called Prompt Health at the beginning of the pandemic. Mental health is not independent of physical fitness. They are interconnected, so taking a step back and looking at the whole person is imperative. I was on a mission to show through different videos that being at your best is not just about your physical body but also about mental, emotional, social, and spiritual well-being. We must care for our bodies, minds and soul.

I started asking people questions by taking them on this journey with me. Guiding them to look within, as we often seem to block emotions and keep going on autopilot. Soon I became known for "Hedieh's Questions."

Now here we are at over 650K friends on TikTok, with many questions asked by me and answered by thousands of people, which I am going to share with you all.

Contents

Understand U

I asked you answered

Hedieh Safiyari

Introduction

The truth is that we often don't want to do self-reflective work consciously. We live life and act the way we act because of what has happened in our past or because it is easier not to think or question anything and let them be. So, what if we give ourselves an invitation for self-growth?

As you go through this journey, know that you give the only validation, and the only answers found are within. When we are more self-aware and present, we start living in the now, the next, and the next.

Use *"Understand U"* as your guide to read and answer questions to understand yourself. Try to be more conscious and aware of everything that perhaps you never thought about, things you always did without thinking twice. Get rid of whatever obstacles may be keeping you from living the life of your dreams. Aim to:

- Be kinder to yourself
- Befriend that wonderful and influential person in your life: You
- Practice sitting with what and how you feel without judgement

When you understand yourself better by exploring different parts of your life, that's when you live and grow to be your authentic self. Lean in and be ready for whatever comes your way. Just as there will be peaks, there may also be valleys where you doubt your abilities or compare your progress with where you think you "should" be. Remember, whatever it is, it is what makes you, YOU. It is your journey, and you deserve to take that next step, whatever you've always desired.

Now buckle up and get ready to explore yourself in a new light:

- Turn the page and read a question and the summary of answers one at a time.

- Perhaps allow yourself to sit with each question for some time—no need to rush.

- Ask yourself how you would answer it differently.

- Be honest with yourself and let it all flow out.

- To answer them yourself, look for the companion book **"Understand U Journal ."** You are given an empty page for each question in that journal to answer whatever works for you. You can write it, draw it or find a picture for it.

- These questions are supposed to make you think about yourself and are great conversation starters with people around you. It can be a way for you to connect with others.

- Leave me a review and share it with your friends. You never know; you might help another person with their journey.

- If you wish to share your thoughts with other people, make a video, put it on social media, and feel free to tag me **@hediehsafiyari**

Now let's start this journey with the questions, and remember, there are no right or wrong answers!

"

May you stay **curious**
Answer **honestly**
Live **authentically**
Love **fully**

"

Q1: What is your name and one thing about you?

"Ever since happiness heard your name, it has been running through the streets trying to find you."

Hafez

There have been a lot of times when someone has asked us, "Tell me about you," whether it is a job interview, a first date, a first time at a social networking or a first time as an author introducing yourself. Often, it might be an awkward or even artificial exchange of names. The first impression is an opportunity to show genuinely who you are and what you are about because it allows us to connect and spark an interest that manifests in unforeseeable ways.

If you were asked this question, "What is your name and one thing about you?" Once you give your name, what would be the next thing you would say about yourself? Is it your personality? Things in which you are proud of or disappointed? Perhaps it may be what you do for a living or how many children you have. Even what astrology sign you may be or your favourite colour.

I asked this question to thousands of people, and this is what was said.

Most people answered about how they are as opposed to who they are. Different words that they used were "happy," "unique," "honest," and "loyal." Some spoke of what they loved and what contributed to their livelihood, like hobbies. Others were happy to talk about their accomplishments, like how many children they have, teaching themselves to do something later in life, and what they own. Others spoke of their pain, like losing someone, being mentally abused, or feeling broken. These hurting individuals found a safe, anonymous place to share their pain.

A few were very confident in their responses; one said they were just as sweet as their name, and another stated they were so unique that they did not have to be in a crowd to be outstanding. One boasted of being in the big league, and another said he was purpose-driven. All this confidence in their answers did not say who they were.

Not too many people chose to or were able to share who they were. One spoke about being a feminist, another an emotional empath, but that was it.

Why is that? Why, when asked this question, people answered how they were instead of who they are? Perhaps from all the answers, some don't truly know who they are or are too scared to share who they are, even with strangers. People come from all walks of life and have experienced things that have changed them, and perhaps that is where the root of the issue of sharing their true selves lies.

After reading this, if you had to reintroduce yourself, how would you do it? If someone you met for the first time were to ask you, "What is your name and tell me one thing about yourself"? Would that make you feel like they care? If so, when answering this, try to be more open about who you are and what makes you, you. Don't be afraid to be curious about yourself and the following new person you were to meet by finding out who they are beyond their sign or their job.

- Be sure to get ***"Understand U Journal"*** to guide you as you answer all these questions.

- Think of the type of person you are. What would you want someone to know you for that first impression? Do you like who you are?

- Come back and answer this question to check in with yourself as you go through this journey.

Now let me introduce myself. I am an Iranian Canadian woman who moved to Canada when I was 16. Living my childhood and teenage years in Iran taught me many things. I was born in 1978, the year of the revolution, and I grew up unable to do many things like other people anywhere else. We were supposed to start covering our hair in elementary school at 9. We were banned from singing, dancing, listening to music publicly, or attending mixed parties. Going to a girls-only school and playing team sports only with girls, I never learned to interact or become friends with boys usually and got accustomed to getting harassed by the morality police for just about anything every time I left the house.

After my adult years in Canada, I learned not to take little things in life for granted. Freedom to walk, talk, dress, celebrate and live like a normal human being is a blessing many people in some parts of the world don't have.

I am Hedieh, and the meaning of my name in Farsi is gift. I was named Hedieh because my parents couldn't have a kid and finally had me after a few years, so I was their gift from God. I am a daughter, a mother, an entrepreneur, and a storyteller. I got the gift of freedom to live a free life halfway through my life, and my gift to you is to remind you of the many things we all have or can strive to have to live a happy and healthy life.

Nice to meet you.

Q2: How's life? How have you been lately?

"People will ask you the question, how is life treating you? But my question is, how are you treating life? On that, your happiness rests."

Rasheed Ogunlaru

You may be asked, "How's life?" or "How's it going?" in different situations, like when you bump into someone you barely know, a co-worker, or even a close friend checking up on you. Many don't think and respond with an automated answer habitually with minimal connection, saying, "Fine." Or can we honestly answer how we are by talking about the highlights of our day? Of course, that also depends on our level of awareness and the sincerity of the question or who it is that is asking that question.

When asked this question, "How's life? How have you been lately?" how would you respond? Would you be quick with a reply? Would you give a one-word answer or a lengthy response? Perhaps it might be something that you would need to sit on before replying. Maybe you might be unable to respond or answer something by habit without thinking about it much.

I asked this question to thousands of people, and these are the variety of responses given.

Many people responded with one-word answers; good, great, sad, lost, but the one that was repeatedly said was "I'm fine." This seemed to be a generic response when one could not put what they truly were feeling into words or did not want to go into details for fear of being judged.

For the most part, though, there were some general responses, ones saying how terrific their life was, how blessed they were feeling, and how at peace they were at this point. But many expressed how much pain they felt, hopeless, discouraged, and so alone. You could feel the intense emotions with these responses.

A lot just responded to the first part of the question, speaking about how their life is rewarding, an adventure, living the dream —also saying how beautiful it was and such a gift. Some believe that giving it your all make it a good day. At the same time, others felt that life was too challenging, tedious, and not worth the effort. Although you can see how they felt with their words, they never said how they were, choosing to focus on outside sources.

A couple of the answers truly stood out. The first is "Life is a succession of lessons which must be lived to be understood." Although this was not giving a window into how they were, this was such a profound statement. Life is filled with lessons personalized for us to grow and learn so that our life can be one that we enjoy living. Another was, "Life has its struggles. Thankfully those struggles are momentary. Focused on the positive." There is much truth in these words because struggles don't last forever, and focusing on the positive will help you get through it all.

One thing that was noticeably missing from all the responses was the mention of another person, family, or friend. Except for a couple that mentioned divorce and a loss of a spouse, no one said having others as a part of their life or how they contribute to it. Was this a conscious decision to leave them out? Or do people truly feel like they are the only ones who can contribute happiness or misery to their life?

I began by asking how you would respond to this question and giving examples of how one might do so. It most definitely can be challenging to answer, especially if you are going through a hard time in your life. But this question can also be a way of connecting with others. By someone asking you this or you ask them, you are making a connection and the more honest you are, the deeper the relationship can be. This can also be true with yourself. By answering this honestly, you can reflect on how you are doing and dealing with your life.

The thousands of people who answered this question allowed themselves to be as vulnerable as they were comfortable. It may not have been exactly how they were or their life, but it's what they were able to share. Choosing to take the chance by sharing some of the most challenging and happiest times with strangers has given them a segue into being connected with other like-minded people and feeling just a little less alone. Whether they chose a part of their lives to share or the full picture, in the end, they still decided to share.

Now that I have taken you through the process and shown you the different ways that people have responded to this question, letting you know that there is no right or wrong answer, how would you react if someone asked you, "How's life? How have you been lately?", will it be easy for you? Or maybe a little difficult? By being willing to answer this question for yourself, you can open the opportunity for growth. Don't you think you're worth it?

- Note anything that might contribute to your current mood and if you can name it.

- Grab your journal, list your typical daily activities, and name one mood in front of each. Cross off the ones that don't feel good and consciously try to do more of the ones that lift your spirit.

- Update this list over time and reflect on it.

While there are moments that are simply outside your control, you can do many things to seize power and feel better. You can take a break, walk, crank up the music, do something nice for someone else, talk to a friend, or do something fun. No one thing helps everyone, so figuring out what works best for you is important. Sometimes you may need more help than others, which is fine. Sometimes you may need to breathe, let go and trust that better days are coming. Responding to how we feel and what we will do about it takes a certain level of awareness. And why does this matter so much? Because once you can connect with yourself deeper, you can connect better with the outside world too.

Q3: When was the last time you laughed out loud?

"The old man laughed loud and joyously, shook up the details of his anatomy from head to foot, and ended by saying that such a laugh was money in a man's pocket because it cut down the doctor's bills like everything."

Mark Twain

You've probably heard by now that laughter is good for the soul. A good laugh is the best way to improve your mood, as helps you to release tension and relaxes your nerves making it beneficial for both your mental and physical well-being. There are many ways to start laughing more often: You can try a yoga laughter group, set aside time just for laughing; maybe it is watching a funny movie, spend more time with others; maybe play a fun game or watch a favourite comedian together, and lastly, "fake it" if you have to. Yes, even a forced laugh will make you feel better.

If you were asked the question, "When was the last time you laughed out loud?" how would you answer it? Would you be able to answer it?

Here are some of the answers given when I asked this question from thousands of people.

The most common response was, "I don't remember." Many could not remember the last time they had a deep belly laugh. Sure, they laughed regularly, but most were done automatically without genuine emotion. Right up there with this answer, though, was "every day." They could find reasons to be truly happy with their actions or surroundings. Something as simple as playing in the waves or watching a TikTok video was able to bubble that laughter up to the surface.

Other answers were a little more specific, like, "not since childhood" or "before covid." While they could pinpoint the last time, going without laughter was still a very long time. Why is that? Why is it easier for some to achieve that deep gut laugh while others find it so difficult to get a chuckle?

Sharing laughter with someone you care about is one of the best ways to connect and create a bond that brings you closer to each other. Most of the answers given included sharing them with someone—some of those included going out drinking and dancing with friends. Just being able to let loose and be yourself is a great release. Another way children just being children brings so much joy is because they have no filter, which can be so hysterical. Lastly, funny movies are another sure way to get that deep belly laughter.

The more comfortable you are with someone, the easier it is to let loose and achieve that laughing-out-loud feeling. Family and friends can be the gateway to this because who else can you feel like you can be your true self around, if not them? The saying, "Laughter is the best medicine," does ring true. Think about it; you're feeling down or stressed to the point that your body is so tense, something causes you to laugh so hard your stomach hurts, and the tension is gone just like that. Never underestimate the power of laughter.

Laughter can be a grounding and healing experience. When doing it the right way, you can't help but be aware of how your body is feeling; it's almost like you can feel the tension leaving your body. Also, sharing this experience with someone you care about deepens the connection and brings you closer together.

I have shown you the different types of responses of the thousands of people who answered the question, "When was the last time you laughed out loud?" I have also given you different views and examples of why laughter is so important to your everyday life. So, if you were asked this question, how would you answer it? Are you able to remember the last time you laughed like this?

- Let's try this laughing exercise:

Reflect on a happy memory during a time that made you feel safe and loved. Now connect with that memory and notice if that makes you laugh.

- Find a picture of you laughing and put it inside your journal, or write up to 5 memories of times when you laughed and allow yourself to feel it.

Making yourself laugh also leads to real laughter, helping you feel better. Remember to laugh, even if sometimes it doesn't feel natural. Remember, happiness is a choice but a daily practice that requires time and dedication, so instead of letting your emotions control you, do the things that make you happy.

Q4: How would your friends describe you?

"Whatever makes an impression on the heart seems lovely in the eye."

Saadi

Knowing what your friends may think of you shows how self aware you are and that you care about what your friends think. That's a positive point for your character and personality. Asking, "How would your friends describe you?" is another question you might get asked in an interview or on a date, where someone is trying to get to know you based on first impressions. Knowing yourself well says so much about you because it shows your character and how you come across to others, whether you know it at all or have ever thought about it.

It takes a high level of emotional intelligence to know that you may have characteristics like being fun, compassionate, a good listener that draws people, or someone with some traits that make people pull away. Whether you share this information honestly is up to you; the most important thing is to be aware of it and do something about it.

If you were asked, "How would your friends describe you?", What would be your answer to that?

When I asked this question to thousands of people, many were able to answer this with at least one thing their friends would say about them. Some of these were: "kind," "distant", "shy," "funny," "honest," and "good listeners," While others were saying "trustworthy," "thoughtful," "and "loyal." There were also some answers like being eccentric, crazy, and topically eclectic.

Others gave some unique answers that showed they are proud of who they are. One of the answers was, "There is more than meets the eye. He is worldly, so don't underestimate him". Another was the "kind of guy you can love and trust as a friend."

Many spoke of not having friends, saying they were "extremely a lone wolf" and flat out that they "don't have friends." Why is this the case? Why do some people find it so much easier to make a lot of friends going through life while others find it more difficult?

After going over the thousands of responses and taking you through the thought process that may go into answering, if you were asked the question, "How would your friends describe you?" what would your answer be? Could you answer?

- Do you criticize your friends or have expectations from your friends?

- Do you to make them feel special?

- Write down at least five qualities you appreciate in your friends. Do you have any of them?

Imagine someone who constantly complains or is confrontational. Now flip the coin and picture someone who has a smile on most of the time, compliments you, is genuinely curious about you and wants to learn more by active listening rather than just talking about themselves, fun to be around and genuinely care. Wouldn't you like to be friends with a person with more positive traits? I bet the answer is yes, and you will say something nice about that person if someone asks you what you think of them. It is all about the vibe, and most of us agree that we would like to be around a positive vibe, so why not be like that yourself?

Q5: What would you tell your younger self?

"Dear younger self, you've always been enough."

Alex Elle

We mature and get wiser with age through different life experiences, meeting different people, travelling, and living in other places. We experience life-changing events, achieve milestones, succeed and fail, and learn from them all. If we knew then what we know now, how could that impact the younger version of us?

Knowing what you know now, you would probably do some things differently if you got a chance. This list may include anything that allows you to explore your full potential and anything that helps you to be at your best physically, mentally, and emotionally. Doesn't that all start with choosing yourself first and getting to know yourself and what you want?

If you were asked the question, "What would you tell your younger self?" how would you answer that?

Thousands of people were asked this question, and these are some of their answers.

Out of all the responses, there were very few negative ones. Some said, "Trust your instincts," while others said, "you're good enough," and "love yourself." There were answers like "never to give up," which you could feel the emotions behind, partly filled with sorrow and a bit of hope. People were very forthcoming with their answers; while the majority were severe and heartfelt responses, there were humorous ones.

Some spoke of things you needed to stay away from or run from. Examples of these are "you're being lied to," which leads you to believe there was much suffering with this answer. Another was, "it gets worse," allowing you to think that this person had a rough start and might not have gotten much better. But the one that stood out, that pulled on the heartstrings was. "Don't give up, as I did," you can feel the pain in that one.

While many of their answers were straightforward and to the point, a few were profound. One was, "Love and truly know yourself before you try to love and learn about another." There is so much truth behind this one because if you don't learn to love and know yourself, how can you do it with someone else? Another answer that stops you is, "Don't be filled with fear. Always choose the choice that scares you the most. It will provide the most growth and awareness." This one shows a deep understanding of the process one would go through with the change.

Some often choose humour to face difficult things; there was no difference here. It can be used to deflect the suffering one might have gone through. One was "to run," run from what? Although this was done funnily, there must be a story behind it. Another that was given in a non-serious way was, "never get old." Why say this when this will inevitably happen? There is no way around it, but this weighed heavily on this person's mind.

I brought you through the answers and showed you the reasons that may have gone into the responses. Knowing all this, if you were asked this question, "What would you tell your younger self?" would you be able to answer it honestly and from the heart?

- Lets try this exercise:

Close your eyes and travel back in time when you were younger. What was your fear? Did you love yourself for who you are?

- Grab your journal and write a letter to your younger self with the wisdom you have now.

Suppose you could talk to your younger self. Wouldn't you want to remind yourself every day is a new day that you can wake up with excitement, not be afraid to try new things, take risks and put yourself out there for new opportunities, love yourself for who you are and love what you do instead of what you could be or what other peoples are?

Life is not a dress rehearsal; we get one chance at it. So, if we got to talk to our younger selves, don't we want to remind them of how they deserve all the great things in life? If I could summarize them all, I would say spread your wings and let your magic shine. Be bold, be YOU.

Q6: What is your #1 non-negotiable?

"The wise treat self-respect as non-negotiable, and will not trade it for health, wealth or anything else."

Thomas Szasz

Non-negotiables are the things you will not negotiate on. They define your values and principles and what you will and won't accept from others and yourself. They are the big-time deal breakers. They are the promises you keep to yourself and those that matter to you. Non-negotiables might be different for everyone- unique to you and your situation; only you can determine what they are and manage them. They are there to guide you through tricky times when decision-making is challenging. For some, they might seem unimportant, while they can be a big deal for others. Maybe it is just simply not working on weekends- family time. Perhaps they are the shared knowledge and rules like not drinking and driving, or maybe they are the principles that are just expected, like not cheating and always telling the truth.

The importance of honesty and loyalty is high on many people's lists. If either is compromised in any way, it can be tough to achieve them again. Having self-respect can help you to keep what is essential to you strong, as well as be able to relay this to others.

If you were asked, "What is your number one non-negotiable?" how would you answer it?

Out of thousands of people that answered this question, these are some of their answers.

There was such a massive response to this question. Every single person that answered was very definitive with their answer. They were not willing to compromise in any way, as they should be. Some of what was said was "hypocrisy," "my dignity," "respect," and "integrity." Others were "freedom," "kindness," "my boundaries," and "my principles." But the most given answer of all was honesty, other things may be negotiable, but when it came to honesty, a lot were saying once the trust is broken, it rarely returns.

One answer was given: "everything is negotiable; there are no absolutes...may not be able to reach an accord but should at least try." Is there something to this? Are we supposed to compromise our values because nothing is certain? While it can be argued that everything can change and nothing stays the same, must we let go of what is important to us because another person doesn't like it?

Another one that was given was "violence" as being non-negotiable. One's faith was another one that was right up there. Individuals were drawing a line when it came to letting go of what they held dear to their hearts. Someone said, "My relationship with Jesus Christ, our Heavenly Father and The Holy Spirit". Also given were "being a devout Christian" and "My faith in the Lord." These were clearly deal breakers to a lot of people.

Something so surprising was some people said that everything was negotiable; there were several of these. How is this so? Does this mean they fly through life by the seat of their pants, where everything is up for grabs, and nothing is important to them? When I saw this answer, the first thing that came to mind was that perhaps one was trying to hide behind something, or they didn't know what it was, so they responded like this. Without boundaries, one's life can be very chaotic, and living like this can lead to an unhealthy lifestyle.

Could you relate as I have taken you through all the different responses? I have shown you how they responded and assessed the reasoning of what might be behind the answers. Many responded with such conviction that the most powerful would not be able to break what's non-negotiable to someone. At the same time, others were not as much and left a lot of leeway with how others can treat them. Now that you have heard all this, if you were asked, "What is your number one non-negotiable?" how would you answer it?

- Let's do this exercise: Think of a list of your top five things which you would not negotiate.

- Grab your journal, and write down your list of non-negotiables and put a number beside each by ranking them in importance. Make sure to keep your list updated as your life changes and share it with whoever it applies.

Being clear on what matters most to you, setting your non-negotiables around that, and following through on them can make a massive difference in all aspects of your life. Boundaries are critical to a healthy and peaceful life that makes you happy. Being able to enforce these boundaries does not make you a wrong person, but someone with much self-respect and love for themselves. The only people upset with this will benefit from your lack of them. Learning to set rules and be on the same page with others doesn't make you any less friendly. It just means you are a high-value individual.

Q7: What is your best discovery?

"At the center of your being, you have the answer. You know who you are, and you know what you want."

Lao Tzu

Life gets busy, and we may lose our authentic selves when we get caught up in jobs that we aren't passionate about or relationships that aren't good for us. Genuinely getting to know yourself is the most critical skill you can ever possess. Once you know who you are, what you need to do and how you should do it, it enables you to avoid frustration by exerting your efforts, time, and energy on something you should not do.

Gaining a better understanding of how you became who you are today can be a wondrous journey of self-discovery. By mining your experiences and inner wisdom, you'll finally be able to answer the question: Who am I?

What would your answer be if you were asked today, "What is your best discovery?"?

Thousands of people were asked this question, and these are some responses.

Out of all the people who responded, very few said they haven't or are yet to make such a discovery. Some spoke of outside sources that helped them to achieve this, while others spoke of finding it within themselves. Examples of these are, "I am the master of my life," "The energy you give is the energy you receive," and "I have a good heart, and no matter how many people have hurt me, I will still have it," and "I'm as forgivable as others." Also mentioned were "being kind to myself and others isn't hard," "that my state of consciousness, not my belief systems, drives spirituality," and "best discovery is me."

A few of them stood out and showed off the place they were at, right here, right now. One was "that anger always comes with powerlessness and losing control. And kindness gives you power and control." This statement was interesting because it shows the yin and yang of the different approaches taken and the outcome. Another was a simple but profound statement, "you can change your life at any time." How powerful is that? You have the power to change whatever you are unhappy or unsatisfied with, you just have to make that choice.

Another that got me thinking was "that the possibility of our next best discovery is just around the next corner when we're open to it." Just surrendering and opening your mind to learning something new can be the connection to bigger and better things. It is all about the mindset and how open you allow your mind to be so that you will find the freedom to continue to learn and grow.

For those who replied with, "nothing still searching "or "waiting patiently," why are they unable to have these discoveries? What is stopping them from achieving this and having the experience that is both freeing and satisfying? Maybe they are not open to it or know how to allow themselves to be. Or perhaps they have found it but are unable to identify it. All it takes is that one moment in time that can change this for them.

Now that I have taken you through all the responses and shown you all the different ways people have answered. Opening your eyes to endless possibilities could help improve your daily life by changing your thought process. If you were asked, "what is your best discovery?" would you be able to come up with something? Maybe there is more than one, which is fine. Sometimes what you are looking for is right in front of your eyes.

- Close your eyes to visualize your ideal self.

- Reflect on what you admire about yourself that is unique to you- it can be a skillset or something innate like your personality.

- Think about what you admire about someone who inspires you.

- Journal your thoughts to create a plan of action.

You may have already considered this self-discovery journey but need to know where to begin. It would be best to start believing in your capabilities, and only you know what they are. Remind yourself that "You are enough," and you have what it takes to do all you want.

You can approach it in several ways by practicing self-love, creating healthy routines, facing your fears and feeding your mind to keep growing every day regardless of your age. It is about changing your perspective and realizing that you are the driver of your success, whatever the meaning of success might be to you. You discover that as you go through this journey.

Q8: What do you think is the most valuable skill on the planet?

"Repeition is the mother of skill."

Tony Robbins

When you think about it, there are endless possibilities when it comes to learning different things you can do to enrich your life, and the most valuable skill can vary depending on your goal. Many skill sets will boost your confidence to live a more meaningful life. They can range from self-discipline, communication, critical thinking, adaptability, emotional intelligence and creativity. The best skill may depend on your unique circumstance and goal. Developing a combination can take you far in life.

You must first understand what you already have, what you are born with, and maybe something you were good at as a child. You might already know this, or you can even ask others for their observations. They are personality traits like being social and bubbly, organized, humour, and positive. They might be talents like singing, drawing, or playing an instrument. They might even be something that has to do with your physical ability, like endurance or flexibility.

If you were asked, "What do you think is the most valuable skill on the planet? How would you answer this?

You might argue that what you consider valuable is based on your life purpose and goal. You might desire to be good at something strictly to advance your career or something that helps your relationships. But is there one thing that can help you in every aspect of your life?

When I asked thousands of people this question, these were some of their answers.

There were many different responses; everyone seemed eager to share what they believed to be the most valuable skill. So many of the answers were about how they treated others, like "communication skill and understanding people's feelings," "listening, really listening," "empathy, not a lot of people manage it nowadays," and "compassion."

Others spoke of learning a tangible skill like "playing an instrument," "foraging," and "the ability to follow instructions." But most of the responses were based on internal learning that helped them to grow as a person and be better. Some examples of these are "kindness, to be kind, even when one is suffering or disappointed to be still kind to all," "curiosity of knowledge," "meditation", "the ability to adapt to change," and "Self-awareness."

A few people said love would be the most valuable skill, but is it a skill? Love is an emotion, a deep affection one develops for another. Love is a learned emotional reaction, but it is not a skill. One of the most given answers to this question was communication. Many people felt that honing this skill would help them navigate life in a way that would benefit themselves and others. Communication is an integral part of our development and helps us grow.

A few of them stood out and showed where they were. One was "using your brain to filter what is right from wrong." When you think of it, you would imagine that everyone should be able to do this, but unfortunately, this is not innate for everyone and comes with high level of emotional intelligence. Another was "being a great leader to ensure peace among all the beautiful people around the world." Reading this gives reason to believe that this person may have experienced such hardship that would leave them longing to develop this skill to ensure no one else goes through it.

After hearing all the examples in the responses, how does it make you feel? Are you able to relate with any of them, or did any resonate with you in a way that made you want to be able to achieve that skill? Perhaps some were able to help set you on the journey to experience the growth and mindset that comes with this awareness. If I were to ask you today, "What do you think is the most valuable skill on the planet?" what would your answer be?

- Let's do this exercise to discover the most valuable skill: Grab your journal and come up with at least five things on your list that you admire: maybe it is something you did as a kid and still do or its something that people you admire do

- Write down beside your list what skill you need or may already have and see what skill pops up or excites you the most, and you got your answer.

A good understanding of our interests, goals, and desires will lead us to acquire skills to help us achieve them. When you reflect on your capabilities and others you admire, you start seeing what you value the most over time. Being better at communication, for example, allows us to control our thoughts and convey them to others better in our personal and professional relationships. Learning something new takes time, effort, dedication and persistence, which is why it requires a good understanding as to why we are doing it in the first place. Once you know your reason and see the benefit, you can put in the time and effort because you know it will be worth it; that requires a high level of self-awareness, and ultimately, that's how you grow.

Q9: What is a dream you let go of?

"When you have a dream, you've got to grab it and never let go."

Carol Burnett

Dreams are important aspirations that give us hope, purpose and motivation to pursue our goals in life. We live in a goal-driven society with "Be all that you can be" and "Winners never quit" mantras that drive us to want to become better and dream bigger. But are we striving to pursue our dreams or something set for us, perhaps by the environment we grew up? Having dreams is a big part of our lives. They help us set goals, plan for our future as well as help us grow as a person. Whatever it may be, it takes work, dedication, and a lot of planning. Dreams are the foundation we build upon to create the life we desire. But it is important to remember first to keep them realistic and be able to change them as we grow.

Letting go of dreams is complex as it means we accept that a cherished goal may no longer be possible and requires us to adjust our expectations. It might include letting go of career aspirations, relationships, or other personal goals. But ultimately, letting go of dreams can also be an opportunity for growth.

If asked, "What dream did you let go of?" How would you answer that?

When I asked thousands of people, these were some of the answers.

Dreams are personal to the individual, and what may be necessary to one may not be to another. There was such contrast in the answers to this question. Most responded uniquely to themselves, but there were a couple of answers that were given by a few, "having children," "finding true love," "love," "happiness," and "soulmate."

This was a great reminder as they are things some of us have and yet take for granted.

Some of the other responses portrayed where the person was in their life, especially when the choice wasn't theirs to make, and they had to accept it and move on. One was, "to feel loved. I probably am loved by my parents, but just once, I wanna feel loved by a woman that chose me. But I don't think that is going to happen". Another was "competing in triathlons, running, being there for my two sons and watching them grow up. That my spouse would take the wedding vows seriously."

However, several people responded that they never had—believing that as long as they are alive, there is always a chance. No matter what life throws at them, they choose to hold on to their dreams in the hope of them coming true. Some of these were, "None, I still have a pulse," "none still working on it," "I don't let go of dreams," and "As I grow, my dreams have evolved, so I haven't let go, just adopted them to my life" and, "I guess none, still dreaming." These individuals are not giving up on them and will believe it can be achievable in the end.

A few answers stood out, having such power in their words and tone. One was "the dream that is the only one that won't let you go to sleep as we are the people who are truly like candies, born to die and give others great memories." Such thought and precision went into this answer, and you can hear the quiet strength in this response. Another was, "as I grow, my dreams have evolved, so I haven't let go, just adapted them to my life." How profound is this? To surrender to the change and accept that things aren't always going to stay the same, you embrace it and carry on.

Dreams are a big part of life; they can fuel us to achieve whatever we want. I took you through all the answers, showing you how one might have come to the answers. If you were asked this question today, "What is a dream you let go of?" what would your response be?

- Let's do this exercise:

Close your eyes, think about the reason behind your dream, and ask yourself if that dream truly is yours or if it is an expectation set for you. Is it realistic?

- Has your dream remained the same or evolved?

- Can you still achieve a dream that would make you happy now? If not, can you let go of it?

- Grab your journal and write down, draw a picture, or find a picture of a dream you can still achieve.

Living a life with no dreams might be like not being alive, as it is a life with no purpose. If our dreams are realistic, there is no reason to let go of them. But it is also important to remember our life may take a different turn at different stages. As we grow, our values change, as does our perception of success or what makes us happy. It makes sense that our dreams can be adjusted too.

Letting go of a dream can be an opportunity for self-discovery, as it may open up new, previously unexplored possibilities. It may also require courage to move forward and find new sources of fulfilment and happiness. Only you know if your plan makes sense; if it does, go for it; if not, don't be afraid to let it go and figure out what you want instead.

Q10: What did you learn from the pandemic?

"Do what you can with you got where you are."

Theodore Roosevelt

The global Pandemic changed life as we knew it around the world. It instilled fear and uncertainty in many people and showed us how strong and resilient we are with all the changes happening. We now have a new norm to which we adapt as we continue life. The Pandemic did a number on the world; it shed fear and panic on vulnerable people, causing so much chaos that it practically shut down the world at one point. We all reacted differently and mostly realized that we couldn't control everything and held on to what we could control the most, which was taking care of ourselves.

As we slowed down in this fast-paced world, we got reminded to focus on things we could manage by taking better care of ourselves. Most importantly, many of us became aware of how much we need other people and appreciate what truly matters: friends, family and connection to others. It was a reminder of how little things we took for granted, like the power of touch or physically being in proximity with other people, makes such a significant impact on our mental health or how much we value our physical health by trying to boost our immune system not to get sick.

If asked, "What did you learn from the pandemic?" how would you answer this?

I asked thousands of people this question, and below are some responses.

One of the top answers to this was the corruption of the government and how everyone became sheep to them during this. Examples of these were "how easy people were converted into sheep," "that there was no pandemic, just government abuse of power," "the manipulative power is greater than I would have ever thought, freedom is just a dream and fear is the ultimate tool!", and "level of government corruptions." You can feel the anger behind these responses, feel how far these individuals felt pushed by this all.

But on the flip side, there were so many positive responses as well, showing what they learned about themselves and others during this time, talking about the growth they experienced and the life lessons they received. Some of the examples are, "nothing is more important than family and health to be happy," "I love and need people," "tomorrow is a gift so go enjoy today," and "create more memories that are meaningful with your family." They chose to see the positive in a terrifying and trying situation that they had no control over, except how they reacted to it.

There was also so much pain and suffering felt during this time, experiencing the loss of loved ones and friends and even losing themselves from isolation and fear.

A few responses stood out: "Many of us struggle alone and in silence. But as we come out of the pandemic, we seek to change that." The power behind these words shows the growth and realization from the suffering felt. Another was, "Adaption and coexistence with difficult circumstances, life is worth holding on to for as long as possible" with these words, you can feel how they chose to see something positive in such a dark time.

Now that you have seen the responses, heard the fear, and felt the strength behind the words, seen that everyone reacted to the pandemic in so many ways and what they did to overcome if I were to ask you, "what did you learn from the pandemic?", what would your answer be?

- How do you care for your body- Would it be healthy nutrition, exercise, or enough sleep? Which areas do you need to address more?

- How do you care for your mind- Would it be by breathing exercises, meditation, music, and getting outside in nature?

- How do you care for your soul- Would it be contributing to the well-being of others, exploring your creativity, or perhaps exploring spirituality?

- Write about activities, draw or find pictures of moments you cared for yourself for your body, mind and soul.

While the pandemic was challenging, it made us grow and recognize what we needed the most. The desire for longing for others and just survival alone made us realize our love for life. The feeling of breathing fresh air with no mask, hugging each other with no fear, and shopping at the grocery store with no pressure were things we had never thought about before. We learned how adaptable we are with many things out of our control, but we still held on. Hopefully, moving back into everyday life as we remember it before, we don't fall back into the same life routine and remember every day is just another opportunity to live and feel alive, not just to exist.

Q11: What does it take to make you feel better?

"It's not whether you get knocked down;

it's whether you get up."

Vince Lombardi

Every one of us goes through difficult times when we don't feel at our best because of the amount of stress we are going through at a time, sometimes, they are short-lived, and sometimes, they last longer. Sometimes they are events we have no control over, and sometimes they are things we can control by removing ourselves from what is causing us a low mood. Either way, it is essential to try and do things that boost our mood actively.

So many things can make you feel better naturally, such as moving your body, breathing exercises, meditation, listening to music or having the right support group. Knowing what works for you best is important, or maybe it is combination of different things. But know that the same solution doesn't work for everyone.

If you were asked the question, "what does it take to make you feel better?" how would you answer this?

Thousands of people were asked this question, and these are some of their responses:

Most people were able to respond to this positively. They could pinpoint their needs and can, find what would help, and take it from there. Some examples of these were: "positive thinking and gratitude to God for what you have at the moment," "working on my best authentic self, for myself first but also so I can be there for everyone else in my life," "positive thinking and thankfulness for what we have now and deep breathing" and "forget yesterday and focus on today." In doing these things, they could move past whatever was bothering them.

Some could not answer this question; they could not give one thing that could help them. Either stating that they don't know or that they tried everything, but nothing worked. What makes it so difficult for them to discover this for themselves? How can they move past their pain so that they can truly heal? It could very well be how they were brought up or past relationships. But it could also be that they are just not ready to deal with it, so they should say, "I don't know."

Others spoke about things that they physically could do to help them feel better, choosing to use something outside of themselves to set the wheels in motion. Some of the responses were "music and reading," "a hug," "healthy gut, sunshine, exercise and good sleep," "checking off things on my to-do list," and "having a nice rest and soaking in a bath." Figuring out what works best for you is the first step, but putting the plan into motion is where the most work is done.

One of the answers stood out because of how it was said. It was a simple line, "it takes yourself to make the changes." This is the truth; only you can choose to take the first step, no matter what anyone else says. If you don't do it, nothing will happen. You are responsible for your actions.

Another was "focusing on what is bothering you most and taking care of it. When it is done, repeat." These two steps can help you get from where you are drowning and bring you to the safety of the shore; if you put in the effort, the only way to go is up.

Having brought you through the responses, showing you the different ways that people were able to get themselves out of a place that was holding them back, seeing all the different ways that they coped with their problems or didn't, if I were to ask you the same question right now, "what does it take to feel better?", how would you answer it?

- Let's do this exercise:

Start a list by answering these questions: Is it scheduling some "me time" to do something relaxing? Is it practicing mindfulness and gratitude? Do you need to ask for support?

- Rank your list to see which one is doable right now and makes you feel better and start with that. Revisit this every time you need to feel better.

Our state of mind affects how we feel and think and what we say and do. Our thoughts may also affect our relationship with our partner and others. Our mental health can also affect our physical health because stress can also affect the physical body and make us sick. Being stressed for too long can affect your blood pressure and cause heart problems. So you can see it is all a vicious cycle, and our mental and physical health is interconnected.

If your mood affects all aspects of your daily life, you don't want to let it last too long. Although we keep hearing, "It's ok not to be ok," we are indeed allowed to feel down sometimes, but it is not ok to let it last too long. You have to consciously try to snap out of it by doing your self-care practices, avoiding what is causing you stress and knowing there is no shame in getting professional help. Many different experts can guide you along the way if needed. Be gentle with yourself, and remember that you can improve things at any point in your life, and you are not alone.

Q12: What text would you send right now if you really didn't give a damn?

"No response is a response, and it is a powerful one. Remember that"

Anne Dennish

Most of us struggle throughout our lives by giving too many unnecessary damns. The ability to reserve caring for only the worthiest situations makes life a hell of a lot easier. But it takes self-control to manage how you care. Sometimes we get confused and feel let down, and it might be tempting to pick up the phone and text whatever is on your mind. However, if you didn't care, why do it?

Hiding behind a phone may serve immediate gratification, but in the long run, it can cause more damage to you than good. The next time you want to pick up the phone and blast someone, think twice because the consequences can outweigh the benefits. Take a few deep breaths. Then, once you're feeling calmer, take a moment to assess whether it's worth picking this battle.

If you were asked the question, "What text would you send right now if you didn't care?" what would your answer be?

When I asked thousands of people this question, these were some answers.

Most respondents said that they would not be sending the text. I could not see the point of doing so if you didn't care. Some thought it would be a waste of time and didn't want to bother with the effort. If you are done with the person, then you're done.

Some said they would send it for various reasons that were important to them. Some of them were, "Can't thank you for much, but I can for the lessons and showing me what I don't want in my life," "I will always love you, but I am choosing to let you go," "there was a time I would have 1000 texts to send. But thank God for therapy", and "I'm sorry, I'm cutting negative people out of my life." These show that the ones sending the text have been through something but are now healing and able to get closure from sending the text.

One answer, just five small words but with such a powerful message, was, "It is what it is." This is a hazardous message because the person sending it is at a place where they have gone through hell and back and survived. They do not care if someone tries to do them wrong because they know they can go through life on their own and have no trouble cutting people out who get in the way of their destination. Once you have reached this point, you are aware of what you need and don't need, and if someone tries to get in the way of your happiness and peace of mind, the door is wide open for them.

At the beginning of this, I went through the reasons why some prefer to text over calling, the different scenarios of how this can play out and the mindset behind it. I also shared that those who chose to text their message were misunderstood. I also went over the fact that if you didn't care about someone, why would you want to send a text? After going over all this, if you were to be asked today, "what text would you send right now if you didn't care?" how would you respond?

Let's do this exercise: Close your eyes and allow yourself to feel what comes to you when you are disappointed at a situation or someone.

- Let's do this exercise: Close your eyes and allow yourself to feel what comes to you when you are disappointed at a situation or someone.

- Ask yourself if you want to share that feeling over the phone and if that makes you feel better.

- Does it worth your energy, or can you be comfortable not sharing it?

- Grab your journal and write your feelings for yourself; allow yourself to forgive and move on.

It takes a lot of energy to care about everything. Please pay attention to where and to who you give them. Remember that life goes on. So, reserve your energy and the number of damns you give to those that deserve your attention. You might be surprised how not giving a damn about everything makes your life much easier and much happier. Any response is a response which means you care, and that is not for everyone. Save your attention and energy for where and to whom it is earned and respected.

Q13: How do you spice up your life?

"Life is short. Break the rules. Forgive quickly. Kiss slowly. Love truly. Laugh uncontrollably and never regret anything that made you smile."

Mark Twain

All of us like a bit of excitement in our lives, and being able to share it with people we care about can make it even more exciting. When you step out of your comfort zone and try something that brings you joy, as scary as sometimes can be, it not only enhances your life as it boosts your self-esteem but can also spill into other aspects of your life. Trying new things and bringing joy to your life doesn't have to be something out of the ordinary. It can be as little as getting out and exploring your city to find little hidden gems, doing a drop-in class for something you've never heard of before or always wanted to try, joining a community of like-minded people, hiking a new trail, taking photos of the sunset, plan a little adventure or go on a wellness retreat to recharge with your friends.

Bringing spice to our lives is stepping outside our comfort zone when life gets routine. It is allowing ourselves to get surprised, learn something new, meet new people, explore new places, having new experiences, and that is a meaningful life to wake up to every day.

If I were to ask you, "How do you add spice to your life?" what would your answer be?

In asking thousands of people this question, you will see some examples.

It was surprising to see by the answers that few seemed to know what this was. There were many comical responses but not very many serious ones. Why is this? What makes it so difficult to answer this? Individuals may have a hard time with this because they might not have experienced it much, and if they have, maybe they didn't realize what it was. Others may have been shy or embarrassed to say because they were worried about what others would think, so they used humour to respond.

Some of the examples that were given that were funny and light were, "I drive an old Toyota with bad breaks," "Just when I cook, I'm spicy enough," and "I need to add ice because my life is already hot," "Indian food," and "I open the cupboard, reach for the jar of chilli pepper powder, sniff generously and enjoy the benefits." While these are filled with humour and are meant to get the readers to laugh, none were anything that would bring the joy of what spicing up your day can bring.

A few of them were given thought to and reflected on the spice they added to their life. Examples of these were, "do what you feel and feel what you do" how profound is that? Being able to allow yourself to do what you want and being present while doing it. Another was "trying new things, expanding my palate, and challenging myself daily with outside-the-box thinking." This would lead you to believe that this person was open to trying new things and wasn't afraid to go out of their comfort zone to bring this to their life.

A couple of others that stood out and showed a lot of thought process going into it were, "I learn a new language or a new musical instrument, I ended up learning 6 languages and playing 7 musical instruments" he put a lot into this and because he enjoyed what he was doing. It worked; he kept doing the same thing.

Another one was "Spontaneity. He is choosing the unexpected. Staying open to new experiences. And a little pepper helps!" With this, you can see that he was always striving to do and experience new things, not allowing fear to direct his path. As well as being open to doing something on a whim with no previous discussion. This often stops someone from doing it if there is no planning done. Of course, a little humour was added to this one in the end, but that could be a little spice, he said to his answer.

After reading the different ways people responded, seeing how a lot of humour was added to answering this question, some well-thought-out responses, and a variety of other things. What would you say if I asked you this question, "How would you add spice to your life?"?

- Take notes of all the small things you want to experience, perhaps things that stimulate all your senses. Does that make you feel excited?

- Write down an idea that brings joy to your life and a plan of action on how to do it more often.

Adding spice to your life means different things to different people. It is considering breaking the pattern and trying something new. Anything that involves challenging yourself, connecting with others or exploring new things or places can make you feel happy and excited to look forward. Life is what you make it, and how you approach it will give you a glimpse of what will come.

When you are excited about something and have things to look forward to, your passion and tremendous energy affect the other people around you, including your friends, relationships and work. So if you've been in the rot lately and feeling bored, it may be time to plan something new to add a little spice to your life.

Q14: What is a piece of advice that really stuck with you?

"If I were a prophet, my prophecy would be happiness. My good news would be freedom; my miracle would have been making kids laugh. I wouldn't scare anyone from hell, and I wouldn't promise heaven. I would teach thoughtfulness and being a good human being."

Charlie Choplin

We all go through life to our rhythm, following the beat of our drum. No paths are alike, showing us something different. Often there are people along the way who impact us, family, friends, and even strangers, and they frequently leave us with words that stick with us for the rest of our lives. Maybe you've heard some heartwarming advice that has stuck with you. But here is the thing, even if you heard something that moved you, it doesn't mean you necessarily remember or followed it.

If you were asked the question, "What is a piece of advice that really stuck with you?" how would you answer this?

I asked this question to thousands of people, and these are some of the responses they gave.

There were so many excellent responses to this; a lot of people were touched by someone that left a lasting impression and words of wisdom. Some of the examples of these were "Better to regret some of your choices than not to have done it at all," "to love someone else, you must love yourself first," "this too shall pass," "learn a little about everything, not all about one thing," and "if there is no sacrifice there is no victory." These fantastic words can bring you to a whole other level of thinking.

Some of the responses stood out to me, and I want to share them with you. There is such power behind the words that show why they impacted the individual that it is still with them today. The first one was, "carefully choose the seeds that you plant in the land of your heart because choosing seeds is easier than uprooting trees." How true is this? To begin with, being careful with who and what you let into your heart is so much easier than letting them go once you open your heart to them. Another was, "learn to accept that you are the villain in someone else's story, don't waste time trying to prove to them you are not." Once someone's mind is made up, nothing you can do or say will change it. For whatever reason, they have chosen this role for you in their life and trying to change their mind will only hurt you more in the end. Lastly, a simple one with such a powerful message, "follow your heart but take your brain with you." It is always ok to follow your heart; it can take you to some incredible places, but always make sure you have your brain with you so that it can help you see what is real or not.

Others that were given that just made sense were, "never trust someone that has nothing to lose," "the lessons will keep happening until it is learned," "If it's meant to be, it'll be easy," "think big, start small," "don't sweat the small stuff, it's all small stuff," "don't cry because it ended, smile because it happened "and "don't compare your chapter one to someone else's chapter twenty." These all give insight into how it is as simple as taking one step at a time, and by not always looking way ahead and staying in the present, you can enjoy the experience more. Tomorrow isn't promised, so living today to its fullest will help make your days more unique.

So many beautiful responses were given that truly inspire one to live the best life possible. I have taken you through many of them, providing feedback on each and showing the powerful message behind each. Now, if I were to ask you the question, "What's a piece of advice that really stuck with you?" what would you give?

- Think of the people who've inspired you in your life with words you hold dear to your heart. Was there any advice that resonated with you?

- Write down one favourite piece of advice you've heard that you think you can start following.

- If it is a piece of advice that more people need to hear, consider sharing it on social media and tag me so that I can share it with others as well **@hediehsafiyari**

Great life advice can lead you to great paths, helping you avoid common pitfalls or offer a new perspective and help you make changes. They become something we like to listen to and feel nice. Although it is nice to hear great advice, we often need to remember them all and never get to follow through with any of them. We have probably all heard touching pieces of advice along the way, but rarely do you hear a piece of advice becoming someone's mantra.

I recently decided to not only collect my dad's wisdom always to remember but also to the extent of making a personal page for it, so they are always there and share them often on my social media channels as well. If you have someone in your life that you admire, you can do the same too. What is more significant than a collection of memories and wisdom from people that make lasting impressions on us as long as we listen and implement them in our lives?

Q15: What's one childhood memory that brings a smile to your face?

"The greatest joys of life are happy memories. Your job is to create as many of them as possible."

Brian Tracy

Childhood memories vary depending on the environment we grew up. We may welcome them or avoid them. They can be uplifting or spirit-shattering. Whatever our age, some childhood memories can still feel painful and honest, and some bring a big smile to our faces. Childhood influences adulthood; our early experiences shape our beliefs about ourselves, others, and the world.

Childhood memories are so powerful. Good ones can make us feel confident & motivated, bring us peace and harmony, and even smile. However, early life adversity is a significant risk factor for developing psychological and behavioural problems later in life. They make up our internal biographies—the stories we tell ourselves about what we've done with our lives. They tell us who we're connected to, whose lives we've touched, and who has touched ours.

If I were to ask you, "What's one childhood memory that brings a smile to your face?" would you be able to answer it?

After asking thousands of people this question, here are some responses.

One thing that stood out with the answers was that so many either didn't remember or didn't have any childhood memories that brought a smile to them. People come from all walks of life, and their upbringing can affect how the image plays in their heads or if they play at all. But what hit home was some of them asking if it was terrible that they didn't have any, like they did something wrong.

Most that were given involved family and friends and things done with them. Some examples of these were "skipping to the first day of kindergarten holding my mother's hand," "when my father taught me how to ride a bike," "spending time with my grandparents," "driving my father's car when I was four in his lap" and "my mom singing songs as my dad drove us kids on Sunday drives in the country." All these show how important it was to have their family with them to create happy memories. Everyone shows their interactions with a loved one and built such deep-rooted memories that they still remember them with a smile.

One was given that although it brought smiles to their face, something happened afterwards that darkened those memories. It was "when my parents were still together." This person may have had many happy memories as a child, but because this painful event happened afterwards, they could not draw on those memories.

The answers that were given ranged from not remembering to some of the happiest moments of their lives. People chose to share a part of their lives that brought joy and happiness, while others couldn't talk about it or didn't remember. There was such a vast difference that it showed that everyone's journey is theirs alone and cannot be compared to another. If I were to ask you this question today, "What's one childhood memory that brings a smile to your face?" would you be able to answer it?

- Let's do this exercise: Close your eyes and try remembering at least one memory that makes you smile. Do you remember where it was? Did it involve senses like smell, touch, taste, or beautiful scenery?

- If you cannot think of a memory that brings a smile, then allow yourself to feel whatever comes to you, accept it, and try to keep the memory from 'the now.'

- Grab your journal and write down whatever thoughts come to you now, or perhaps find a picture of it to keep in your journal.

Often the childhood memory that comes to mind can tell much about us. Sometimes we may not consciously or subconsciously want to remember a lot, or nothing comes to mind. Depending on the memory, we may block them until there is a trigger, and that's when they overflow, and we each deal with it differently. Some can deal with it independently, and others might need extra help.

Reflecting on childhood memories puts a smile on my face. They might be moments that bring about strong emotions we never forget. I remember the first time I biked with two wheels. My dad took off the training wheels and pushed me off. I was scared but so excited. It was right in front of our house when I was five. I remember screaming, laughing, and crying out of excitement because I did it for the first time, and it wasn't that bad. It still makes me smile when thinking of something I did for the first time. Your experience and memories are part of your life. The past is a part of your story, good or bad, and many seasons of your life are still coming up.

Q16: What is the nicest thing someone has ever done for you?

"Even small acts of kindness can make a profound difference to somebody else."

Misha Collins

Many small acts of kindness can make your day, like when someone stops to let you take a turn in the height of traffic or when someone helps you with a heavy box in the grocery store or lets you go first to the cashier if you have fewer items, when you receive a random compliment from a stranger, or when someone smiles and says, "hi."

Kindness is an action linked to enhanced feelings of well-being. Anything that involves empathy and compassion brings you happiness and lowers your stress. Helping others can give us a high level of life satisfaction by improving our mood; it is called "Helper's high"; when the brain releases feel-good chemicals.

If you think those things are lovely, wouldn't it be nice to return them to someone else? Imagine if these small things make a big difference in someone's life; how would it be if there were much more important things that could change someone's life, like being given a shelter or help when in need.

If you were asked the question, "What is the nicest thing someone has ever done for you?" how would you answer this?

After asking thousands of people this question, the following are some of their responses.

A few people said they couldn't remember the most incredible thing someone did for them. Some stated that they were the ones who did this for other people and were not comfortable having it done for them. They felt that it was their place to do it, have always done it and wouldn't have it any other way. At the same time, others stated that there was nothing that someone did for them that was nice. Is this truly the case? Or was it that they didn't want to share? Perhaps it simply was that they couldn't remember and, for whatever reason, could not draw on that memory.

Some of the answers were based on what was given to them. They felt that was the most incredible thing ever done for them. Examples of these are, "I took my two daughters to a Steak House last Saturday. I asked for the bill, and the waitress said, "don't worry, someone paid for your dinner," "sending a driver with a bodyguard to pick me up from a remote office in Nigeria," "saved my family and me from the aftermath of Hurricane Katrina. Put us up in a house and help us", and "the wife gave me a child." All of these done for the person were able to give them the memory of someone caring enough to do something for them.

We also had some very heartfelt responses about how people accepted them as they were, loved them, and listened to them. Some examples of these are, "when my daughter looks me in the eyes, smiles and says, "I love you." Then I know that it's for real.", "My parents have never let me down, always supporting me in everything I do," and "accepted me from the start, no questions."

These individuals were loved and supported, and they never wondered if anyone cared. Knowing that there is someone who loves you unconditionally is one of the best feelings ever.

One of the responses that stood out was, "my business partner embezzled our company one month before I was getting married. I was broke, but she married me without a doubt of our future and life together." This one right here is the best demonstration of unconditional and true love. It did not matter to the woman that the man she was about to marry had just lost everything. This shows that she truly loved him for who he was, not what he had —such a testament to love.

Now that I have gone through some of the given responses, I showed how one could feel like something nice was done for them. I was bringing you the conclusions made as to why some of the answers were given as they were. If I asked you this question, "What is the nicest thing that someone has ever done for you?" how would you respond to it?

- Have you ever received an act of kindness that has changed your life? Was it something small or big? How did that make you feel?

- Write down some kindness you have received and if you have tried any of them for others, and how does that make you feel helping others?

If you've ever received a "pay it forward" moment, you already know that the simplest gesture could completely change your day, especially during a difficult time. Instead of paying someone back, you pay it forward to create a chain of goodwill. If you still remember a moment of kindness and how that made you feel, I bet you agree it is rewarding when you do something nice for others. Next time we encounter something that requires patience, let's be more mindful and always remember to be kind.

Q17: When did you know it was over?

"Once you give up, you know you are done."

Gerald Green

We've all experienced tough times with those we love and occasional arguments are usually nothing to worry about in healthy relationships. At some point, however, you may face a feeling of doubt that's hard to ignore. Maybe you've lost your connection, or a problematic event has damaged your trust. Maybe you feel no emotional connection, the physical intimacy doesn't appeal to you anymore, or other people start to seem more appealing, you have so many disagreements, the trust is gone, or the goals don't align anymore. You may have drifted apart. So, how do you know if the relationship is over?

If asked the question, "When did you know it was over?" how would you answer it? Could you answer it?

When thousands of people were asked this, these were some of their responses.

The most common answer to this was when they found out their partner had cheated on them. Some are together for years and discover that the one who was supposed to love them unconditionally decided to get intimate with someone else. This must be one of the most devastating ways to find out. Some didn't

63

even try to hide it; that would have been a punch to the stomach. Knowing that you have gone into the relationship with your whole heart, taking your vows seriously, and then finding out they were not, would tear anyone apart.

Some were based on their behaviours towards them, ending with something so unforgivable that there was no return from it. Some examples of these are: "he left me alone in the hospital when I was in labour," "he refused to come to my only brother's wedding after being in a relationship for ten years," "When she became aggressively worse, in a short time, with the controlling and abusive behaviour," and "he didn't call or text me when I texted him that my mom had passed away, that was my husband." These were heartbreaking because they weren't there when you needed them the most and never showed any support.

Other answers displayed how they became emotionally distant, not showing any interest in them and leaving them emotionally while they were still there. Some of these were: "I discovered his ego was more important than my mental health," "I made her lasagna when she got home, and she took it without a word and went to sit in the other corner of the sofa," "her constant Facebook posts never included me, and she was obsessed with how she looked, even though I told her she was beautiful," and "I asked for help, and he didn't help me and was never happy for my achievements." All these would bring anyone to their knees when the one person you thought you could count on, the one that was supposed to help you feel complete, disappeared. That must be so hard to be there daily with them physically but having them emotionally distant.

After reading all the responses and seeing the different ways, the responder finally knew it was over. I could identify that this was the end, and there was no coming back from it. When I ask you the question, "When did you know it was over?" how would you answer it?

- Consider some warning signs you noticed affecting your trust, communication and connection.

- Write down a moment or list of events that led you to believe it was over and name your feelings.

- Have you come to terms with what you feel or still need help?

Knowing a relationship is over can be difficult and complex and may involve several factors, including lack of communication or intimacy, dishonesty, loss of interest, unresolved issues, etc. Every relationship is unique, and knowing when it is over can be difficult.

Finding yourself lonely is never easy, regardless of what's causing a disconnect in your relationship. If you're still in love and want your bond to last, you might seek counselling to communicate better and understand each other. All relationships have obstacles—before you give up, try finding new ways to get past conflicts in a healthy way for you both. Remember, we all change and evolve; it is normal not to change simultaneously.

Q18: What's one thing you haven't said out loud?

"If you can't explain it simply, you don't understand it well enough."

Albert Einstein

Sharing something out loud, even to yourself, requires introspection and self-reflection. It could be a secret, fear, desire or a thought you have hesitated to express for whatever reason. Of course, you don't want to share your secrets publicly or with just anyone. It's liberating to acknowledge how you're feeling or what you're thinking by confessing it to yourself.

Even those who have no trouble speaking up and show little fear still have things they have never spoken out loud. So much is behind this as to why someone would do that. Fear of judgement is the biggest; not knowing how others will react can silence the strongest people. There is something powerful about saying things out loud, even if it comes out in writing. Not only pen to paper but through the keyboard or even texting.

If you were asked the question, "What's one thing you haven't said out loud?" how would you answer it?

When I asked thousands of people this, these are some answers.

The top response to this was, "I love you." So many people have felt this and could not say it to the one they loved. Something stopped them from saying it out loud, and now some are living with the regret that it's too late.

Some of the answers had to do with someone who was a part of their past and how they felt in the present time about it. Here are some of the examples of that, " I did the best I could at the time, I love you," "it's not my fault I was a child," "I hate the narcissist I wasted thirteen years of my life on," and "as bad as it was and as crazy as it sounds, I sometimes miss her, or who I thought she was, and that I feel guilty for thinking that. So messed up, I know." These individuals may be anxious to say this because they could feel that it shows weakness on their part or that no one wants to hear it.

Others were heartbreaking to read because you could feel the anguish in their words. A couple of these were: "I feel so guilty for not saving my brother because I didn't believe he was as bad as he was. Biggest regret", and "I miss my fiancé and my daughter; they should never have been in the car, it should have been me." So, heartbreaking to read these words; the pain that the individuals felt seemed to have cut them deep and still remain with them today.

Others chose to be vulnerable with what they shared and gave us a glimpse of the struggles they were going through. A few examples of these are, "I'm depressed, that shows weakness and men are not allowed. So, we carry on because, well, life", "in the closet for four decades," and "sometimes I fear the parts of me that are broken might never fully heal." It took such bravery to share these, and what an example they are setting for those who read it because it may make the reader feel a little less alone.

After reading the answers and seeing the courage those responding showed, I saw the pain, the regrets that were felt and the love that was lost. If I were to ask you the question, "what's one thing you haven't said out loud?" would you be able to answer it?

- Put your hand on your heart and allow yourself to feel the heaviness of what you've been holding inside.

- Write down the feeling that comes up.

- Now say it out loud to yourself. Maybe even scream it. Try it right now if you have not yet!

- Was it loud enough? I hope you feel better.

Words that went unspoken for whatever reason: fear of rejection or judgement, or feeling alone and that no one would care what they had to say; whatever it was, the courage to write them for a bunch of strangers was tremendous. Awareness and acknowledgement are the first steps instead of shutting down or numbing yourself.

Holding on to thoughts, feelings, and even body sensations can weigh us down or create negative emotions that are not good for our mental health. We want to say many things; some profound, some remarkable, some shocking, some gentle, and some life-changing. Some are intentional, and others are accidental. Some are truthful, and some are not. Letting go can be scary. But all are important in their way. Whatever it is, don't let it bottle up inside you. Let it out and allow yourself to heal as you acknowledge whatever you've been holding on to and need to release. You'll feel so much better. If you are struggling to identify something you have not said out loud, journaling or talking to a trusted friend or therapist who can help you explore your thoughts and feelings in a safe and non-judgmental space may be helpful.

Q19: If someone tells you that you are "almost perfect," how does that make you feel?

"Our perfection lies in our imperfection."

Sandor Ellix Katz

We all like nice compliments as it makes us feel seen and appreciated. You might have been in situations where you felt intense things, but you weren't sure about the feelings or what was happening, and for some reason, you pulled the brakes so abruptly. You get the impression that someone is great, but something is missing. Remember, it takes two to tango. It is always two different perspectives according to two different life experiences. There is something that makes the compliment "almost perfect."

How would you answer the question, "If someone tells you that you are " almost perfect," how does that make you feel?" what would be your response?

I asked thousands of people, and these were some of their answers.

The responses to this question were interesting. While there was a number that did not get a good feeling from this kind of compliment, the majority were ok with it and didn't see anything wrong with it. Some of the women's comments who did not care for this one were, "give a compliment then take it back. Not very nice", "Don't accept that. That's caressing your ego and bringing your insecurities to surface.", "He wants to shape you. It's a selfish tactic. RUN", "I would not like it one bit; it would not make me feel good at all," "Why almost? What made you say that? Who are you to judge my worth? How am I supposed to feel?", "Where is this going? Pretty much would be full of questions, and I don't think I would feel good" and "shitty because you know the criticism is coming." These people felt judged and like someone was trying to mould them.

For the most part, men did not see anything wrong with this question. They believed it was ok to compliment someone like this and could not see why it would upset them. Many felt there shouldn't be negative feelings toward this question. Examples of these were, "good enough for me, it's a compliment to me," "feel good especially when the one who said it is special to your heart," "it would make me feel good," "it is one of the best compliments. We all have flaws and shortcomings, even if they aren't seen at the start of a relationship," and "I feel proud and responsible to keep such a good compliment always."

As I brought you through various responses and showed you the differences between how the women answered and the men, what were your thoughts on that? Did you agree more with one side over the other? Or did you not have an opinion either way? From reading all the answers, you could see the divide between the sexes and that there was no middle ground. If I were to ask you the question, "If someone tells you you are "almost perfect," how does that make you feel?" what would be your answer?

- What would you feel when you hear you are "almost," knowing it means "not quite"? Does it bruise your ego, or will you listen to it as you are not "quite the right match"?

- Write down the feelings that come up and how you feel about them. Is the person who is complimenting you "almost" perfect to you? You might be surprised that there are "almost" always mutual feelings.

Men and women are psychologically different, affecting our personalities and social interactions, including giving or receiving compliments. Women often receive more compliments and, as a result, are more sensitive toward what they get, while men might not receive as many compliments and might accept any compliment.

When you encounter a person with whom you are not quite the right match, you must listen to your gut feelings and remind yourself it is not always about you. The word "Almost" goes both ways; otherwise, you would have been a "Perfect" match. After all, you want to be where you are celebrated for everything, being with someone who sees you as "perfect" and them to you with all the imperfections we all have, which is called love.

Q20: How do you know real love?

"I love you neither with my heart nor with my mind. My heart might stop. My mind can forget. I love you with my soul because my soul never stops or forgets."

Rumi

When you have butterflies in your stomach, feel giddy when you see someone, daydream about your life together, and think you are in love. But wait, is it love or lust?

Lust is the honeymoon stage when you are still discovering and learning about each other purely physical. The high can feel like an addiction and consume all your mental space; it's when you are infatuated and don't see any flaws. It can turn into love, or it can end after a while. Whereas love is that compassionate care for someone beyond that. When someone truly loves you, they drop their expectations and see you as you are. When you see someone, your eyes light up, and you feel joy, which will never fade. After the honeymoon, it even gets stronger; you get more comfortable sharing all parts of yourself, all the imperfections, by being yourself without hiding, still feeling calm and secure. True love is all parts of any great relationship wrapped in one.

How would you answer if you were asked today, "How do you know real love?"?

This question was asked to thousands of people, which are some of the answers were given.

Out of all the answers given, few said they didn't know what real love was. There was a wide selection of how they believed you knew it was true love, but in the end, the vast majority thought they knew. Here are some examples of what was said, "when it's time-consuming, it's a ridiculous kind of feeling you can't live without," "chemistry, it's that simple," "when nothing is required," "When you can look at someone, see all their imperfections and despite them, still see them as your person and want to spend forever with them," "real love is a mother's love, the true unconditional love," and "real love starts with mutual respect, followed by some common values. You go into it not thinking you will change the other person. Acceptance." As you can see, there were all different kinds of answers here, and none were wrong.

As I mentioned, there weren't many answers that said they didn't know what it was or didn't exist. Examples of these are, "no such thing; they all come with an expiry date," "you don't know because it doesn't exist," and "you don't know because there's no real love anymore. Love is money these days". The tone you could feel by reading these words makes you wonder if they believe this or that they just haven't experienced it yet, leading them to believe it doesn't exist.

The top answer that both men and women replied with was that you don't know what real love is; you feel it. When you think about it, it does make sense since love is an emotion and emotions are felt. A few examples of these were, "you don't know real love, you feel real love," "It starts off spiritual and manifests into intellectual attractions," "you don't know you feel it," and "you don't know, it's just a feeling of deep happiness." The way some of these answers were written, you can't help but believe that it truly is something that is felt and not just known.

In the responses, it was argued that you couldn't know real love but that you feel real love. After taking you through all the answers and displaying the different ways that people view it, if I asked you, "How do you know real love?" what would your response be?

- Let's do this exercise: Close your eyes and remember a time that you felt this immense feeling, something that stoppted you in your tracks.

- Was it a single moment or series of events that led you to believe what you are feeling is actually love? Or was it lust?

- If you had to express genuine love, could you? Write in your words how you describe true love.

True love is sometimes mistaken for excitement and butterflies in your stomach. As exciting as it is, it may be infatuation that turns into love if you are both heading in the same direction. True love means consistently showing up, not just when convenient, and going out of your way to show someone you care. True love doesn't give up on you. True love hugs you when you are angry; when you don't answer calls, they still come to you; when you get insecure, they remind you how important you are and when you want to leave, they remind you this is where you belong. True love is not supposed to be hurtful or possessive. It's accepting, and fulfilling. You can cultivate this quality of love by reshaping how you see yourself within the equation. It all starts with you. You must love yourself first to give and accept healthy love to and from others.

Q21: Have you ever asked yourself what your purpose in life is?

"Life without a purpose is like a body without a soul."

Tasneem Hameed

Finding your purpose in life is more than a cliché. Living a life with purpose can lead to a sense of control, satisfaction, and just feeling happy. Can you relate to that?

Without meaning, you won't feel content because you don't feel aligned with the things you do. Living a purposeful life is different for everybody: maybe it is providing for your family, making positive connections with others, travelling the world or something else. It comes down to setting a goal to feel a certain way: to feel loved, to be happy or to have a positive impact on the life of others. Are you doing that already?

If you were asked this question today, "have you ever asked yourself what is your purpose in life?" how would you answer it?

After asking this question to thousands of people, these were some of the responses.

I was surprised to find that there were quite a few of those that answered that they did not know what their purpose was in a life or had even asked themselves this. They could not draw on one thing that could say what that purpose was; why is that? Some of the examples of this were, "I've been there many times, but I can't find it, so I'm sadly living my seemingly happy life, seeking out my better half," "yes, and I still have no idea what it is," "I asked myself that so many times but I'm still clueless, and I'm seventy years old," "Since I was fifteen. Apparently, I have big problems communicating with myself, or I'm probably deaf", and "Yes, and I'm still waiting for the answer."

The next one right up there was their faith. Those who answered this had varying ways about how their purpose was intertwined with their beliefs and did not believe that it could be interchangeable with anything else. Examples of these were, "to serve my God. Everything else is a bonus. Only starting to listen at fifty-two", "no I leave it up to the good lord, he will guide me if I lean on him. Never lose faith", "to share the glory of God, the creator," "to worship Allah. To do good things and Allah will give us Jannah after our death", and "as Muslim, our purpose is clear and rich to that we have done our best with people and choose the best things for ourselves." These individuals have such a deep-rooted faith that they have found purpose through their faith.

Others answered that they had asked but did not give an answer. Was this a conscious decision? Or was it so private to them that they did not want to share? These examples were, "yes, I have it!", "Good question, and I did," "yes, I have. The answer is crystal clear", "Everyday! It shall not be revealed", and " Yes, and I think I found the answer." As you can see, it's clear that if they did know, they could not share for whatever reason.

Still, many responded that gave some valuable answers that showed insight into who they were. The examples for this were, "yes, to reach others, to spread kindness and laughter. To teach, be happy and healthy, to be a superb mama and a creative human being", "stay happy and spread happiness and love," "To inspire others through my writing and to share my experiences. Also, to continue working on being the best version of myself", and "to find happiness and peace of mind."

As you can see from the answers, this journey is very personal; it is not something you can take from someone else and use as your own. What would your answer be if I were to ask you, "Have you asked yourself what your purpose in life is?" what would your answer be?

- Answers these questions to yourself:

What do you enjoy doing? What are you good at? What have been some of your most meaningful experiences? What kind of life do you want to live? What kind of person do you want to be? What inspires you? What kind of impact do you want to make?

- Bring all these together to write your purpose in your journal.

It may not be easy initially when you begin this journey filled with self-discovery. There could be confusion or even doubt, but if you remain focused and use your determination as your drive to find the truth, the results can be so beautiful and unique. Ideally, your aim should blend with what interests you and brings you joy. In Japan, this idea is known as ikigai, the concept of following your pleasure. It would help if you had a sense of purpose to sustain you over time. And even when life feels like a series of compromises, you can still discover and connect to your goal by exploring what brings you joy and dedicating more time to it.

Once you discover your goal, you'll find that your life opens up in ways you never thought possible. You will experience new depths of opportunity, and your eyes will open to all the possibilities around you, and by that, you can feel fulfilled and happy.

Q22: What kind of animal would you be and why?

"It's better to live like a lion for a day than a jackal for hundred years."

Tipu Soltan

Everyone's personality match with the characteristics of a specific animal. Your spirit animal could be anything from wild tigers and wolves to cats and dogs. Some are quiet and confident, while others are strong and free. Some are a symbol of courage and strength; some are a symbol of loyalty; some represent love, while some show purposefulness or cheerfulness. Your admiration of one animal over another speaks volumes about your personality and character traits.

We are the product of a unique combination of influences; our genes, upbringing, training and our living environment. And these differ for all of us, making us unique. Many of us come into contact with animals every day, but have you ever wondered which matches your personality? Are you very social and friendly, and they call you the life of the party or quiet and peaceful?

What would your answer be if you were asked, "What kind of animal would you be and why?" what would your answer be?

Out of the thousands of people that were asked, these are some of their responses.

One of the top answers that were given was a horse. So many people could relate to being solid and loyal, which is precisely how a horse is. Some examples were "a horse, free-spirited, serving and majestic," "horse because I'm humble," "horse, strong, loyal and speed," "horse because it's strong and loyal," and "a horse because they seem to give smiles to sick children." Being able to relate to a horse lets people allow people to see themselves as the beautiful, strong, and loyal person they are.

Another one that was up there was a dog. They felt the connection because their needs were like theirs. Examples of these were "dogs because they are loyal," "German Shepherd, they are smart, independent and they love steak," "dogs, loving, loyal, friend," "dog, want always to protect my loved ones," and "dog, specifically Labrador because I love to rescue people and animals." From these answers, you can see that loyalty and protecting loved ones are critical to them.

There were a few that were unique, and you would not think to compare yourself to them. But the responder felt a connection to them because of what they represented. Here are the examples of those, "Dolphin, intelligent, social so never alone, enjoy playing and free to travel to some beautiful places," "penguin, because it doesn't have a clear identity, just like me, has wings but can't fly and walks on two legs but find it difficult to move, and can't be alone," and "I think I would be a water bear, they are one of the most resilient animals and can weather any conditions, extreme or mild, that would otherwise destroy another animal." How awesome is it to look within yourself and see all these beautiful qualities that compare to some of the most majestic animals ever?

I started by showing the comparison that you might have with an animal, listing off the strengths and traits they have that you could relate to. There are so many beautiful animals out there that radiate the same feelings and values that we have, and there are many people who speak of how they have a spirit animal because of how much the person relates to and admires. If I were to ask you today, "what kind of animal would you be and why?" how would you answer it?

- Think about your personality and skills and answer how you view yourself as a human being.

- Now, either write, draw, or find a picture of the animal you would be and put it in your journal.

If you are unsure and wondering how close you are to what you already think you are, there are quizzes you can take online to show you what animal you would be, based on your personality.

When I reflect on my personality, a horse is the first thing close to my heart. Horses are friendly and generous, so that they can make many friends. They can carry a heavy load when needed. Independence is also their strong point, as they can survive many obstacles.

Q23: If you could do it all over again, what would you do?

"When you arise in the morning, think of what a precious privilege it is to be alive, breathe, think, enjoy, and love."

Marcus Aurelius

We all might regret what we didn't do or wish we had done some things differently. It can include mistakes made in careers, friendships, and relationships. Making mistakes is inevitable, but let's learn from them instead of regretting them. Look at it this way: many lessons can enrich our lives at any point, like not taking the moments for granted, taking better care of ourselves, spending more time with those that matter, and choosing people in our lives carefully.

Sometimes we blame external sources because of where we are now. There are always things we can't control but many that we can control. The reality is our self-imposed restrictions affect our ability to create change. Instead of thinking of excuses for why certain things happened or didn't happen, we should accept responsibility for our choices and change the ones that don't make us happy or proud anymore.

If you are asked the question, "If you could do it all over again, what would you do?" how would you answer this?

I asked thousands of people, and there were some of their responses.

It was interesting to see that very few people said they would change anything; although their life may have been difficult and they experienced a lot of pain, they would still not want to change a thing. Some examples of this were: "I would do it again because I love what I do because I am convinced of what I am doing in my life.", "This is a hard one because, on the one hand, there are those things I would think I would want to do over, but on the other hand, these experiences made me who I am today, and I love that person," and "my life, pretty much the same. It's been a phenomenal journey, both ups and down but still quite fun." These individuals felt that although their journey was not all rainbows and unicorns, they wouldn't change anything because it made them who they are today.

Other answers were more about how and what they did, stating that they would do it differently if they had the chance. Examples were, "not ignore the red flags and stop making excuses for her," "spend less time trying to succeed for my family, and more time with them." "Go into my son's room even though he seemed asleep and talk to him like we were doing. Maybe stop him from killing himself" and "not getting married." As you can see from their words, there are a lot of regrets because when looking back, they realize that if they had done it differently, the outcome would be different.

Some spoke of internal decisions they wish they would have made, believing that today their lives would be much better. Examples were "live my life mindfully" and "stress less." Notice how it all has to do with you mindset.

I began this by talking about regrets and the toll they can take on someone. It also showed you the different examples of what they would do differently if they had a chance, highlighting the emotions that came with it. Now, if I were to ask you, "if you could do it over again, what would you do?" how would you answer it?

- Reflect on some of your lessons learned.

- What is the first thing that comes to your mind? Have you healed, or does it still hurt?

- Write down the details of what you would do differently.

Everyone makes mistakes and chooses to do something they sometimes regret seconds later. We all have dreamed of correcting that one thing that caused pain. Not all of us will get this chance, but how you let it affect your life ultimately counts.

Think of a new day as a unique chance. A chance to start all over again and do things how you always wished you did. Another opportunity to have the courage to turn around. A chance to be yourself before you worry about meeting others' expectations. Are you willing to give yourself that chance? The answer has to be out of pure instincts, and I hope it is a screaming one, like "Hell ya," with no doubt.

Q24: What's stopping you?

"The only thing stopping you is fear. The only thing that will get you past it is courage."

Steve Pavlina

We often second-guess ourselves and miss opportunities for new possibilities. Every time you want to start a new path, change a situation, try something you like, make a decision or open up, fear of "worsening the situation," "something going wrong," "Getting judged," or "Being called selfish," or other self-talks might stop you. Think about all the subconscious thoughts that play in our minds daily; doubting ourselves can gradually chip away at our self-belief.

Not to suggest we can do anything and everything we want, but we can acknowledge that we can work on our self-talk and adopt the right mindset. Despite all the fears, take a moment to imagine if you could stand up and allow yourself to move forward and tackle whatever you choose. How does that feel? Do you feel empowered?

How would you respond if you were asked the question, "What's stopping you?"?

I asked this question thousands of people, and these are some of their answers.

The most given answer was "yourself." So many people acknowledged that they were stopping themselves from taking a chance. They let the voice get to them and put a wrench in their wheel to move forward. Some of the examples of these were "myself", "I used to be the one stopping myself, and now I'm my biggest motivator," "me, myself, and I," and "I am, trying to fix it."

While some were able to move past themselves as a hurdle, others are still trying to work on it so they aren't standing in their way anymore.

Other responses were based on how one was feeling and how that was stopping them. Examples of these were "my poor mental health," "fear of failure," "more than often not, fear of judgement, but I'm working on it," and "Fear is a big barrier. But slowly breaking through and learning to take chances and gain wisdom", and "crippling anxiety." The most common word used was fear; it was the most crippling emotion that didn't allow them to move forward.

There was one surprising answer that was also given quite a lot: "nothing." They felt they could do whatever they wanted and had nothing holding them back. Some of these were, "Nothing, I am unstoppable. If I was stopped in the past, it was 'me'", "nothing is stopping me, I am the only one who can do it," "good question, the answer is, absolutely nothing," and "absolutely nothing, I never tell anyone my plans, always moving forward." As you can see from these responses, they were able to find a way that helped them to be able to tackle whatever they wanted.

Some spoke of not having enough money, which was what was stopping them, believing that they needed that to succeed with their choices. Others talked of their childhood trauma, how the pain from it all these years later keeps them stuck, not allowing them to move forward.

You have now read through all the examples given by those who responded. After seeing what they wrote and the struggles or victories they had, you see that most were aware of what was stopping them and had decided to act. If I were to ask you this question today, "What's stopping you?" how would you answer this?

- Are you aware of any negative self-talk, and do you challenge it?

- Do you practice positive self-talk by focusing on the present moment?

- Create a list of your favourite affirmations and create an action plan by writing what it takes to get there.

We all have self-imposed beliefs that stop us. We create this brick wall or maybe even an anchor holding us down. Once we look within to see what is holding us back, we often find that our obstacles are excuses, thinking we are not enough or lack confidence, knowledge or resources. There are usually a million excuses that we can think of. The most common would be blaming someone else or "Only if I didn't do that," Sound familiar? Are these stopping you, or are you using them as excuses?

Here is a challenge for you. Why not challenge ourselves to challenge whatever is stopping us? Let's do it from today. The challenge is "No more excuses." No one is going to hand your dreams to you. It is you rooting for yourself, and only you make it happen.

Q25: Would you continue dating someone when you both know there is no future?

"The heart says yes, but the mind says no."

Albert Einstein

You meet a person with everything you have been looking for: great conversations, shared values, lots of laughter, support, and great chemistry, but there is no future. There is a battle between the heart and the mind to stay or to leave. Depending on where you are in life, settling down might not necessarily be on your radar or is it? The heart might say to enjoy the company, and the mind thinks long-term.

Your heart's passion and your mind's wisdom are great gifts, but the logical and the emotional sides are at odds and often don't agree. Your heart encourages you to take risks, leading you to passion and beauty, which logic could never predict. But the heart can also be naive, ignoring rational thinking.

If you were asked the question, "Would you continue dating someone when you both know there is no future?" how would you respond?

When I asked thousands of people this question, these were some responses.

The most likely answer to this question was, "mind says no, heart says yes." This short answer is packed with so much confusion. The number of people who could relate to this was enormous, each with their own story of a love that maybe shouldn't have been. It's like there is an internal war going on that is beating up the heart and silencing the mind.

Another well-liked answer was "Carpe diem. If they add to your life, even for a season, then yes." Some were willing to give it a go because they believed in making the most of the present time with little thought for the future. The benefits outweighed the risk, so it was worth it to them.

There were so many that said yes. They were willing to stay in the relationship and were ok with dealing with any consequences if they were to arise. Some examples of these were, "Yes! Because you must live in the moment and not in the future. Life is too short! Choose to be happy", and "yes, live in the present; good memories are not a waste of time," "yes, some people are just fun. Have had great times with people I knew weren't going to be forever. Why miss out because of expectations?" and "I can only say yes!" Each one has decided that living in the present is more important than worrying about the future.

As well, there was an overwhelming response to the answer no. They were unwilling to give up their peace of mind to hang onto something that would not last. Examples of these were, besides the many that just answered "no," "NO way! Life is too short, and you should be with someone you are with every day", "When I don't see him in the future, no," and "no, mind over heart." All decided that their mental health and well-being were more important than maybe.

I have shown you the overwhelming responses that bounced between yes, and no, and the heart says yes, but the mind says no. They have taken you through what might have been going through their mind based on the tone of their words and gave you many examples of the different mindset people have while making these choices. Now, if I were to ask you this question, "Would you continue dating someone when you both know there is no future?" what kind of answer would you give?

- Evaluate their values and if your values are on the same page by answering these questions: Are they kind, respectful and honest? Are there common interests and activities?

- Write down what stage of life you are at and your goal before you answer.

How you deal with a situation where you have to decide whether you are wasting your time by spending it with someone there is no future with can depend on where you are in your life. Some decide they have something to gain from every relationship as long as it is good company and adds to them, even in the short term. Others won't even give it a second thought and will move past it with little resistance.

The truth is every experience serves a purpose and allows us to learn more about what we don't want long term in our life. Having a goal of sharing a lifetime or the rest of our life with someone can be a worthy and beautiful goal. If you choose to spend a part of your life with someone with no future because you are experiencing what you need at that time in your life, then let it be; as long as you are not modifying your dreams, you are not sacrificing your wish, and you feel fulfilled.

Q26: Do you think you can change people?

"Change how you look at things, and the things you look at change."

Wayne Dyer

Making changes isn't easy and doesn't always follow a straight path. But that doesn't mean people don't change. People change only when they want to and are self-aware, receive support, and become intentional about behaving differently. And even then, change takes time and may sometimes be challenging. A few things impact a person's ability and desire to make changes in life, including their genetics, motivation and personality. We can't make someone change, but we can only be there to give support. When someone goes to the extent of getting professional help, it shows a genuine desire to change beyond empty promises.

If you were asked today, "Do you think you can change people?" what would your answer be?

I asked thousands of people this question, and the following are some responses.

Many of the answers to this question were no; they did not believe that someone could be responsible for the change in another person, no matter how much they wanted it. If the individual was not ready, it wasn't going to happen. Here are some examples of the responses, "Change? No, help them see a way to grow and potentially support, absolutely", "no, and you're in the wrong relationship if you think you can," "I can inspire by example. Change, to be effective and possible, must come from within. Anything forced lacks authenticity", and "you can give them thoughts and direction, but the bottom line is, it's truly up to the person." As you can see, these individuals believe change is possible, but only if the person wants it.

There were two most liked answers, and although they were similar, they brought different levels of understanding. These were the answers, "Absolutely not! The only one who can change a person is the person. However, you can be an inspiration for the change", and "I think you can inspire, but change is up to them." They both were evident that they believed they could not change the person, but it didn't mean they could not support the change. Helping one to realize that they want to change is one of the most powerful gifts you can give them.

Now there were a few of them that believed that you could change someone. By offering advice and guidance, they thought that change would happen. Examples of these were, "yes, of course, once you give someone advice that touches his soul, he will change," "yes, you can change people with new things and lots of love," and "we can if we do it with all our heart and put effort. They truly believe that change will happen if they love them hard enough. But will it? Is it going to be a natural transition if other forces it?

You have now seen the different responses that were shared, the divide between believing that you can change a person, as opposed to inspiring and supporting them. There has been talking that you can change them with enough love and support, but it has also been said that you can inspire them, but you can't do it for them. When it comes down to it, if someone wants it bad enough, they will make it happen without being coerced. What would you say if I asked, "Do you think you can change people?"?

- Recognize it is not your decision to change someone; you must accept people for who they are.

- Write down the best support you can give someone who wants to change.

If we choose to have someone in our life, we choose them for who they are and not what we wish they become. If we want them to change into the person we want them to be, they are not the person for us. But sometimes you don't choose some people in your life when the person is your family member or blood-related.

We have to remember if a person wants to change, they will attempt to learn new behaviour to achieve their goal. As much as we love to help our loved ones change for the better, we can't do it for them, but we can motivate them and create a supportive environment. We can only encourage them and let them know that we will be there to be their number#1 cheerleader and that they are not alone.

Q27: If your ex wanted to rekindle the relationship, would you?

"Happily ever after is not a fairy tale. It is a choice."

Fawn Weaver

There is a saying that 'an ex is an ex for a reason'; this belief comes from the fact that never has a breakup happened without a rift, no matter how much you have worked through it since. While this is true, there are still some that think that people do deserve second chances. But before you do this, you must consider what will be different this time.

Many people consider re-entering former relationships because they already know what they are getting. Perhaps some awareness is created during the time apart, each person taking responsibility for their shortcomings. Rekindling is only possible if you have taken the time and have done the work to grow and heal from previous scars, can forgive and don't bring up the past.

If you were asked, "If your ex wanted to rekindle the relationship, would you?" how would you answer?

Thousands of people were asked this question; below are some responses.

Hands down, most of the answers were a resounding no! They were not even going to give it a second thought because what broke them up was so painful that they didn't want to go back there. Some examples were, "no, I lost all respect for her, and I'm more than she has to offer." "No, it did not work once; the odds are that it will not work on a second trial," "Have to remember the reason they are your ex," "nope, I burned my hands once touching a stove, I won't be touching it again.", "No thanks, my ex tossed me out of the house like cold turkey, without trying marriage counselling," and "she did/does, but what caused the breakup was too damaging to me to take a chance at reliving it. Upward and onward." As you can see with these answers, what ended was so damaging that no matter how they felt about them, there was no chance because there was no coming back from it.

There were a few that, although they said no, spoke of how it ended on good terms. Examples of these are, "no, my ex is an amazing person, but there were many core values that we did not align on. The breakup spared us years of conflict", and "no, simply because it was beautiful while it lasted, and we still respect each other. If we stayed together, we would not have that respect." These individuals choose to take the positive from their relationship when remembering it, and while they haven't forgotten why it happened, they are in a good space and don't want to ruin it.

Surprisingly some said yes; they were willing to return to it because of the love, even though it was painful. These are a couple of examples: "yes, if we were both honest and willing to put in the work and new skills needed. I'm still in love with her", and " yes, we get along better now than after seventeen years of marriage." You can hear the love through these words; they acknowledge there were issues but are willing to give it another go in the name of love.

I started by saying that an ex was an ex for a reason and went on to show you some examples of these. Also, I brought you through the different responses, giving insight into the answers. As we saw, the majority were entirely against getting back together, stating the damage was deep and there was no coming back. If I were to ask you right now the question, "If your ex wanted to rekindle the relationship, would you?" how would you answer that?

- Ask yourself if the relationship is fixable. Can the trust be rebuilt again?

- Have either or both of you changed for the better?

- Write down if you would consider rekindling the relationship and how you wish it could look.

You may need to ask yourself if getting back together is for the right reasons, remember the problems in the first place, and avoid falling into the same old patterns. It could work if you go about it realistically and emotionally healthy. You can strengthen your relationship. The requirement is for both people to be on the same page and focus on what they've learned and how they can become better partners by leaving the past in the past and moving forward.

Q28: What is one thing that you love about yourself?

"Talk to yourself like you would to someone you love."

Brene Brown

Self-love means kindness, compassion, and accepting yourself unconditionally and without judgment. It involves taking good care of your needs, desires, health, and well-being. Loving yourself will give you self-belief, self-worth, confidence, happiness, and positive thinking skills. It gives you the mental toughness to pick yourself up after every failure and keep trying without thinking about giving up. It gives you the power to look past disappointments and frustrations and live positively. It offers you the strength to ignore negativity.

Hearing about the benefits and importance of self-love might make you wonder, "why such a big deal for something so simple and natural?" We can sometimes be our worst critics, doubters, and judges. Loving ourselves is the most important thing, as it is the foundation for all our encounters, from work to relationships affecting all aspects of our lives. Because if we don't love ourselves, how can we expect someone else to do it? Self-love starts with self-awareness, knowing what we appreciate about ourselves.

If you were asked this question, "What is one thing that you love about yourself?" how would you answer?

I had asked thousands of people this, and some of their answers.

It was a pleasant surprise to see that out of all that responded, very few said nothing, and they could not articulate what they loved about themselves. It may not be that they didn't at all but were finding it hard to express. However, the rest showed a wide range of what they loved, some were about their appearances, but most were about how they felt.

Some examples of these were "my ability to get up when I fall," "I love life and try to enjoy it every day," "my love for my children, it keeps me going, I want the best for them," "I love that I have the strength to pull myself out of anything and be stronger and happier than before," "faithful with all my heart," "my willingness to help others," and "I am open to all people in the world, we are not so different." As you can see by the responses, what they most loved about themselves was how they tackled life and treated others. Being able to do the work within and use that to reach out to others is such a beautiful and selfless act.

The most common answer was that being compassionate was what they loved most about themselves. Being willing to look past the differences and embrace them, always have a kind word ready to share or a smile. Examples of these were "my kindness," "I have a good heart," "I'm a good friend to a fault," "my ability to really listen and then to speak or not to speak," "my big heart," "my compassion is great," and "my caring heart for others." These people wear their hearts on their sleeves and, by showing love and compassion to others, increase their love for themselves.

There were so few answers that said they didn't love one thing about themselves, and so many that were able to name off at least one thing that was amazing to see. The path one takes to find self-love can be long and winding, but as you saw from some of the examples, so rewarding in the end. If I were to ask you this question, "What is one thing that you love about yourself?" how would you answer?

- Start a list of everything you love about yourself, including your personality or particular abilities.

- Consider how you affect other people.

- How long is your list? I bet it was longer than you expected. Use this list as your daily affirmations.

When you look within and find things you love about yourself, it shows growth and strength. And you don't need to be perfect to love yourself. Self-love is the act of embracing yourself with all your shortcomings and imperfections. Finding your way to self-love is a journey that may have a lot of ups and downs, but as soon as you reach your destination, there is no better feeling. Once you can love yourself, you are free to spread it to others, and the spark is much stronger when the message you are giving is one that you believe in yourself.

Q29: What would you do if you had one billion dollars?

"Free is a man who has no desires."

Nizami Ganjavi

Having a lot of money is many people's wish. Some believe if you have a lot of money, you won't have any problems. Others view it as a safety net to navigate through life. The more money you have, the more secure you will feel. But will you? Will it provide a safe landing when all hell breaks loose?

We're never satisfied. We always think, "if we just had a little bit more money, we'd be happier. Sure, money "fixes problems," and the reason money increases happiness up to a point seems to be that having a certain amount of money helps to fix specific problems that make people stressed out and unhappy. But once you meet basic human needs, much more money doesn't create much more happiness; perhaps more stress and responsibility come with it if we live a conscious life.

Our answers vary depending on our priorities and values and how we want to use our resources to impact this world positively.

How would you answer if asked, "What would you do if you had one billion dollars?"?

Out of the thousands of people who asked this question, here are some of their responses.

Most answers said they would use them to help others and ensure their loved ones are set for life. Examples of these are "a lot of humanitarian activities for the unfortunate, educational fund, employment, housing and health services globally," "care for my family and take care of a whole lot of veterans," "I would feed the poor people, build houses for the homeless and I would pay off my sister's house loans," and "make some donations to the poor because we won't take anything with us when we die one day." Doing good actions is what people would remember, and "make my family and friends secure; then I would start a foundation and help people." All these answers spoke of how they would help others, and not one was how they would use the money for themselves.

Some mentioned the worldly things they would buy and what they would do. Some said to travel, while others wanted to buy houses and invest. Some examples of this were, "I would buy a small log cabin in the middle of nowhere, by a lake, and get a dog and a trustworthy truck," "pay off debts, get a car of my choice and a home in Portugal," "invest it," and "buy a small tropical island and create a sustainable community dedicated to living disconnected from society." They believed that acquiring these things would make them happy and would be able to live a full life.

A few answered that they didn't want the money; they didn't believe that having that money would bring them happiness and could bring them a lot of misery. These examples were, "I prefer to be happy" and "I would rather be happy and comfortable than be rich and miserable. I know there is a lot you can do with the money but is it worth your happiness? I don't think so", and "I would not like that much money, happiness is worth more." When it comes down to it for these individuals, their happiness is much more valuable than a billion dollars.

I started by talking about the benefits of a lot of money, what people could do with it and how they might feel. I then brought you the answers to what was given and showed you the contrast between what they would do and how they would feel. Then went on to portray those who said they wouldn't want all that money because their happiness is more important. If I were to ask you right now, "What would you do if you had one billion dollars?" how would you respond?

- How much of your money do you spend on yourself?

- How much of it involves helping others?

- Can you help others in a way that doesn't require a lot of money?

- Write down a list of things you would do and notice how much of it is for you and how much is for others. That says a lot about you.

We all have different goals and values. Some of us might have always dreamed of starting a business, travelling or exploring the world, maybe you want to buy properties and invest your money, or perhaps you want to help others and donate to a charity. Ultimately, we use a way to achieve our dreams to feel happy. If you want to know how to use the money to become happier, you need to understand what brings you happiness in the first place.

Of course, what you spend money on could be things, experiences, or both.

Consider the other things that make you happy aside from all the money in the world. If you got a billion dollars, but tomorrow was your last day, would you accept a billion or want more time? If your answer is time, ask yourself how you spend that time. Are you caring for yourself and others, learning, growing, and smiling? So many things to be happy for without a billion dollars.

Q30: What would you stand for if you knew no one would judge you?

"To be unafraid of the judgment of others is the greatest freedom you can have"

Timothy Shriver

No one is as worried about what you are doing or saying as you are. Because they are concerned more about their lives and their worries, people may have heard your story but can't feel what you are going through; they aren't living your life. Sometimes you are holding your life back because you care so much about what others think or the judgement they might place on you, and often we judge ourselves even more.

Fear of judgement doesn't allow us to live an authentic life because we can't be true to ourselves. But let's be honest, how often the fakeness of some people has bothered you? Don't you appreciate someone genuine? Living an authentic life affects all aspects of our lives because we know who we are, and aligning ourselves with our truth is more effortless.

If you were asked, "What would you stand for if you knew no one would judge you?" how would you respond?

Thousands of people were asked this question, and these were some of their responses.

Out of all the answers, the vast majority replied that they had already stood up for something and did not care what people thought. Judgement wasn't something they feared because if they felt strongly about something, someone else's opinion didn't matter. Examples of these were, "my voice is loud on injustice. I never cared about what others say. It's my life, my journey", "I would stand for everything I do now, I could care less who judges me, except God," "I am already an activist in a few different political arenas, and I thoroughly enjoy it," "I pretty much do it now for my community," "At my age, judgements don't bother me, I've always stood against bullying, in any form," and "I stand for whatever I believe in regardless of the sheep that judge me." By reading these responses, you can feel the passion and drive behind the individuals and the dedication to what they believe in.

Some also spoke of what they would like to stand for but have not quite gotten there, but had they had no risk of judgment; they would be right there fighting. Some examples of these were, "I'd be a fearless Christian, but I'm weak, so God helps me," "I would stand for a better life all over the world, regardless of race and religion," "I would stand for liberty and justice for all," "freedom," and "honestly, decency and care for my fellow humans." These are all amazing, and sadly, that judgment is a factor that stops someone from what they believe in.

A quote that comes to mind is 'if you stand for nothing, you fall for anything' by Alexander Hamilton, speaking of the importance of decision-making that is led by your core values. This is so important here; those who are letting fear of judgement from others might be allowing those individuals to compromise what is important to them. Finding your voice to raise awareness and joining others to make them louder is what the world needs more of.

After seeing all the responses and showing the different ways people either already do or want to stand for, you can better understand their reasoning. You heard the passion and determination behind the words when they spoke of what they believed in and stood for. If I were to ask you right now, "What would you stand for if you knew no one would judge you?" how would you answer?

- Reflect on your personal values and beliefs and answer: What is important to you? What motivates you? What drives you to do the things you do?

- Consider the things you like to but don't or can't do.

- Write down what you know is right for you and if you would continue to do even if no one else was watching.

Our upbringing, culture, experiences and personal preferences shape our beliefs and values. Feeling Judged can be the loudest silencer. Reflecting on what you would stand for if no one judged you, you may gain some insights into your true desires and values and find ways to live a more authentic and fulfilling life.

Remind yourself that no one pays as much attention as you think; even if they do, it is temporary. They have their own lives to worry about. And what if they judge you? There will always be judgments. The more you know about yourself and act in a way that aligns with what matters most to you, the quieter those voices will get, and the bolder you'll be able to be in your own life. Living truthfully and authentically gives you more profound freedom and happiness. When you can boldly be you, it affects all aspects of your life, including your interactions, relationships and overall well-being.

Q31: What does success mean to you?

"To laugh often and much; to win the respect of intelligent people and the affection of children; to appreciate beauty, to find the best in others; to leave the world a little better; to know even one life . has breathed easier because you have lived. This is success."

Ralph Waldo Emerson

Success means different things to everyone. For some, it can be achieving financial stability or fame; for others, it may be personal growth or helping others. Defining your definition of success and striving towards achieving it in a way that aligns with your values and beliefs is essential. Success is not about achieving a particular milestone but the journey and the positive impact you can have on yourself and others around you. By not drafting your definition of success, there's a high probability that you're pursuing someone else's definition.

We all grew up differently, some with cultures and environments that your profession defined success. Remember the question we all got asked as a child about what we want to be when we grow up? How many of you answered doctor, engineer, lawyer, and others? Was it because it was what your parents wanted, it was considered successful, or did you know what you wanted? Are you happy if you have your ultimate job or all the money in the world?

If you were asked this question, "what does success mean to you?" how would you respond to this?

Thousands of people were asked this, and next, you will find some of their answers.

There were very few responses that spoke of money or worldly things. Of course, some were financially stable, but nothing else. Does this surprise you? We live in a highly materialistic world, where most people are concerned with what they have and not who they are. But does this change as we dig deep within?

Out of thousands of responses, not one listed what they had.

Most of the answers were about what they can do to better their lives to become mentally and emotionally stable. Some examples of these were, "to do something new successfully, that's a challenge for me," "success to me is pursuing joy in life, regardless of the traumas and trials of life that tempted us to quit," "success is having the freedom of choice and ability to do your actions without restrictions," "Knowing I did everything I could to achieve living my best, healthiest, happiest life I possibly can, and sharing that joy with others," "success is balance, equilibrium," and "Knowing how to deal with people, the rest is just icing." The mindset of these individuals is quite apparent, and you can feel the underlying determination and pride in their words.

One of the responses that stuck out and made me take a second glance to capture the message was, "Success has always meant one thing to me. I'd like you to think about this for a moment. You can't see the back when the fridge is so full." How profound is this? Do as the responder said and think about it, not in a literal way, but figuratively. How wonderfully successful would you feel if your life was so full that you didn't need to look elsewhere to complete it? Knowing that because of your hard work and determination, you built a life you were happy with and never want to escape. Isn't that the ultimate success?

You have now been brought through the responses of all the responders; been given the insight into what success meant to them and why; were able to hear the strength and determination in every word written, feeling their pride and joy. If I asked you this question today, "What does success mean to you?" how would you answer?

- Answer the following questions:

Are you pursuing goals that you find meaningful and passionate about? Are you making a difference in the lives of others? Do you feel loved and understood? Do you have the respect of family and friends? Are you doing work you love? Do you laugh often? Are you happy? Are you healthy?

- Bring all those answers together and write down how successful you feel and what it takes to get there.

Success is subjective and can be influenced by personal values, beliefs and goals. There is no single measure of success, and certainly no single answer for how to be successful in life. But as we saw from the answers to this question, success doesn't mean the same things to people. Despite your thoughts, success isn't determined by what you have. It's more about who you are and the energy you put out there. Success has become more about your self-worth and not your monetary worth, as you can have all the money and shiny things in the world and still not be happy. If you answered yes to most of those questions, I would guess you are living a successful life.

Q32: If you had the world's stage, what would you want to be known for?

"All the world's a stage, all the men and women merely players."

Shakespeare

We can make a meaningful difference in this world every day and they don't have to be grand; we can do so in small ways. Many problems need solving, but life can't be just about solving them; they need to inspire us to make us glad to wake up every day and be part of humanity. Don't you think so?

Acknowledged for something you hold dear to your heart can be the ultimate gift. Knowing that you are making a difference in someone else's life could help them and yourself. As humans, we have a nurturing nature and the need to make sure others are okay, which can be powerful.

If you were asked this question, "If you had the world's stage, what would you want to be known for?" what would your answer be?

I asked thousands of people this, and some of their responses.

Most of the answers were about what they could do for others. Being able to make a difference in someone else's life was very important to them. Examples of these were, "the one who builds bridges between people and cultures" and "I want to inspire and help people lose excess weight. My message isn't about diets or recipes, but the mindset one needs to have to do something so difficult", "for helping and supporting others and always choosing kindness. Building people up, not just women, and being a safe person for people", "being kind and humble, no matter how rich I can or will be," and "I would propose a plan to end hunger, poverty, and make sure all kids have access to education." Every single one of these individuals would find great pleasure in being known for how they treated others.

There were others about how they can make someone feel; some examples of these were "leaving them with tears and belly aches, from laughter," "my sense of humour," "making people smile," and "compassion." Helping someone feel better in any way they can is essential to them and would make them happy to be known for it.

Some had more of a personal approach that involved improving life for themselves and not just others. These examples were "that I dance every day and am blessed with friends I want in life" and "the best I can be." When you are at your best, this also affects those around you.

The most liked answer that was given showed the responder's strength and compassion. It was "sharing kindness, love and making people laugh. Laughter is the best medicine" as you can see, being able to deliver to another the best medicine was something that brought them joy. Ensuring those around them felt loved and wanted was their fundamental goal.

Now that you have read the responses, felt the emotions behind the words, and seen the amazing things that people desire to be known for, see the many answers that show just how much love and strength that have fuelled them; if I were to ask you this question today, "If you had the world's stage, what would you want to be known for?", how would you respond to it?

- What motivates you?

- Does your motivation make a difference for others?

- Grab your journal and make a list of what matters to you and want you want to be known for?

We all have different motivations that drive us. It can range from independence, security, power, respect and recognition to the opportunity to grow and make a difference. Sometimes we can influence others by doing little things in life, like making someone laugh and sometimes, depending on our resources, we can do bigger things, like creating more peace for everyone. Sometimes our passion naturally drives us with no previous plans. Your energy ensures that the message you want to convey hits where it is needed. When you think about it, every day, the world is our stage that we can use however we want to make a difference, even if it is a small one, if we live a conscious life.

Q33: If your life had absolutely no limits, what would you do?

"There are no limits on what you can achieve with your life,

except for the limit you accept in your mind."

Brian Tracy

Many of what seem to us as limits in life are only limited to our mental selves. If you think like this, you free yourself from all the limitations. Life is just a story; all that matters is how hard you imagine and try to achieve your dreams. Whether it's something for yourself or others, the options are endless. We can do many things to have a meaningful and purposeful life. You can explore and achieve anything you ever wanted, pursue your passions, become an expert in a field, travel the world, see different cultures or learn new languages, and push yourself to reach your full potential. Imagine walking up every Monday morning full of energy, excited for every hour ahead. What is the point of living for Friday?

Not to say anyone can do anything, but we have so much control over how our life pans out. Limits can serve as motivators and help us learn and grow. Challenging ourselves and not settling for the easiest option is always more rewarding. So while it is great to think of a life with no limits, we should still appreciate the value the limits can bring to our lives.

If you were asked, "If your life had absolutely no limits, what would you do?" how would you respond?

This was asked of thousands of people, and these were their answers.

Out of all the responses, the majority were on what they can do for others or how to make the world a better place. Being able to make someone's day just a little better or easier is something that brings joy to them. Here are some examples of these, "if I were lucky enough to fulfill my dreams, I would share my fortune with others," "to make sure no one around the globe went to sleep hungry," "first to make sure my family is taken care of, and to help the people in underdeveloped countries," "spread kindness, peace, happiness and motivation as many people as I can," and "I would remove all the conflicts between the nations, put peace and banish hunger from the planet." These individuals feel that making the world better, one person at a time, will make their lives happier.

Quite a few spoke of what they would do for themselves, what they'll buy or do. Examples of these were, "I would have the ability to fly around the world in my aircraft," "having the right woman and enjoying every moment, cherishing her presence in my life to my last breath," "a log house deep in the forest on about 500 hectares", "flying into space for all discoveries to the end of the universe," and "the love of my life and I travel the world and have adventures together." Although these were about things they would do or get for themselves, when you think about it, if they are happier, they will project happiness onto others.

One that stood out did not say anything about what they would do for themselves or others. It was, "If you remove the struggle, the wanting goes away. Limits are necessary to move the spirit."

This is a simple yet powerful answer. This individual believes that to appreciate life and draw on its wants; we must struggle first. How else would we understand what we achieve without experiencing pain and heartache?

Various answers were given; some would want to do something for themselves, but the majority was what they could do for others, especially the vulnerable. The thought that went into each response was precise and quite admirable. If I were to ask you today, "If life had no limits, what would you do?" how would you answer it?

- If you knew there were no limits to what you could be and achieve, would you still be doing what you are doing?

- Write down a list of things you always wanted to do and if you are doing some of them already.

- Update the list every time you consciously do something new.

If life had no limits, the possibilities would be endless. There are many ways to pursue our lives, including seeking our passions, challenging ourselves, learning and growing daily, and helping others. We are born into a world full of opportunities to explore. However, we might not all pursue that curiosity to reach our full potential. Everyone has their perspective on their life. Limits are sometimes by the external environment we live. We can create many people in our minds and push beyond them if we dare to discover who we are and give every aspect of our uniqueness to the world. That's how we get to live extraordinary lives.

Q34: What was the bravest thing you've ever said?

"What's the bravest thing you've ever said?" Asked the boy

"Help," said the horse

Charlie Mackesy

Being vulnerable is not easy. Opening your heart and telling something private, personal or bold takes a lot of courage. The fear of rejection or judgement prevents many people from speaking things out loud to others. It takes courage to be truthful sometimes and takes practice to be brave. It is daring to be vulnerable, but it is what helps us transform and grow. Vulnerability can be uncomfortable and scary, but it is a powerful tool for personal development and growth, as help us to build stronger connection with others and develop empathy and compassion.

If you were asked this question, "What was the bravest thing you've ever said?" how would you answer?

After asking thousands of people this, these are some of their responses.

The two top answers were 'no' and 'I need help.' These individuals were at a place in their life where they had to speak up and say two of the hardest things to say. A couple of examples of these were, besides "no," "Like many others said no, saying no is sometimes a brave thing to say!", "When I called a therapist and asked for help," "I need help," and "I am sorry I can't do this right now." They could speak up and tell someone their boundaries and what didn't work for them, quietly demanding the respect of accepting their answer in return.

Another common one was asking for a divorce. You had to speak up and tell the person you were married to that it wasn't working and that you needed to part ways. They are taking the step to make a significant decision in their life that can be so scary and confusing. Examples of these were, "I can no longer stay in this relationship because none of my needs are ever met, even though I love you so much!" and "after raising my kids and respecting my marriage for twenty-six years and accomplishing my mission and responsibility of living a peaceful marriage, I asked for a divorce," and "I filed for divorce."

Others' responses were things they said but also what they did. Some examples of these were, "told my friend I liked her more than a friend," "I said I'm going to jump out of an aeroplane to raise money for charity," "I do," "married my wife in a private non-church ceremony," "I made a mistake, it won't happen again," "I deserve love not abuse. I know it's hard with two kids, but you can do it and leave a thirteen-year relationship. Best decision I ever made!". A lot of strength and courage were felt from some of these words.

When I began this, I spoke about how being vulnerable was not easy and then gave examples of how people showed this vulnerability and the strength and hard work that went into this. These answers showed some rawest emotions and fears; the respondents let us see their mindset. If I were to ask you this question today, "What is the bravest thing you've ever said?" how difficult would it be for you to answer?

- Think of a personal experience when showed courage in words.

- Reflect on inspirational advice on courage.

- Write down what bravery means to you.

We all have different experiences and perspectives on what constitutes bravery. Our truth may be something about ourselves or something that has to do with our external environment and has to do with others. Allowing ourselves to be open and show others a side of us that is difficult to share takes a lot of courage and vulnerability. We don't know how they will respond or if they will even care what we have to say. Even the simple but powerful statement 'no' or 'help' takes so much effort that it can often cause the individual to reconsider and not say anything. The power of vulnerability allows you to live your truth without the fear of judgment, to be authentic, be bold, and be what makes you, YOU.

Q35: What is your favourite colour? Why?

"Shine is my favourite colour."

Marc Jacobs

Do you feel anxious in a yellow room? Does blue make you feel calm and relaxed? Artists and interior designers have long believed that colour can dramatically affect moods, feelings, and emotions. "Colors, like features, follow the changes of the emotions," the artist Pablo Picasso once remarked.

Colour can be essential in conveying information, creating specific moods, and even influencing people's decisions. Colour preferences also affect the objects you choose to buy, the clothes you wear, and how you may even furnish your place. We often select objects in colours that bring out certain moods or feelings, such as choosing a car colour that seems sporty, futuristic, sleek, or trustworthy. Room colours can also evoke specific moods, such as painting a bedroom a soft green to create a peaceful mood or dressing in a classy and professional way, like black or soothing like white.

How would you answer this if asked, "What is your favourite colour? Why?"?

Thousands of people were asked this, which are some of their responses.

The top answer that was given was blue. There were a lot of reasons that were given as to why, but overall, it represented calmness to them. Here are some of the examples, "blue, because it reminds me of my childhood back home, laying in the grass staring up at the sky," "blue, it's the ocean, my sanctuary," "sky blue, it's soothing, and it relaxes me," "My place where the land meets the sea," "sky blue like the clouds because I feel at peace with it," and "blue for me because it feels bright, fresh, pure and gives me hope." As you can see from these responses, blue gives them a feeling of tranquillity, which is crucial to them as they navigate through life.

Another one that was up there was white. So many people loved white because it gave a feeling of cleanliness and order. Some examples of these were, "my favourite colour is white because I associate it with cleanliness," "while studying at school, one day our teacher told me that colour is compelling and contains all colours. It's true for me", "white because it stands for peace," and "white because it always looks fresh." Most seemed to actuate the colour white with power, feeling that it represents someone in control of their life.

Other answers that were given were an array of colours, and some of the reasons behind them were pretty interesting; examples of these were, "sakura pink. Shows a beautiful beginning and end, for they only last for a moment", "green, I associate it with nature and my love of nature," "yellow at all shades, it reminds me of the gold value of life and the energy of the sun," "orange, bright and happy like the sun," "black because it reminds me of the night sky," and "Minnesota Vikings purple. I think because when I was a child, I thought it was fun and pretty and still a boy's colour. I was afraid to like pink". Many different colours seem to make people feel a certain way based on a memory or association with something special.

You saw how each colour meant something different to everyone, even when choosing the same one, as well as their importance of them. If I were to ask you right now the question, "What's your favourite colour? Why?" how would you answer?

- Do you have a colour preference? What colour clothes do you keep in your closet mostly or what colour furniture do you have? What is the colour of your car?

- Grab your journal with coloured pens or pencils and draw something with your favourite colour.

You may or may not have a favourite colour. But if you notice a repetition of a particular colour in your choices, this can reveal your personality. Colours can influence how we feel and act. These effects are subject to our personal, cultural, and environmental factors. So, the next time you are about to meet someone for the first time, consider how you may want to be perceived. The colour you wear next time to that interview, first date, or the video you post on social media says so much about you.

As I reflected on this exercise, I noticed a lot of white around me. I started searching the terms used to describe white, known as delicate, calm, fresh or pure. I can relate to calm and its simplicity. I remember hearing from a designer, "It is not right unless it is white." And this brings a smile to my face as I say it.

Q36: What does the perfect day look like to you?

"And one perfect day can give more clues for a perfect life."

Anne Morrow Lindbergh

A perfect day can look different for all of us depending on our interests, personality and priorities. Everyone has ideas of what their perfect day would look like. Some may say spending it with loved ones, while others might choose solitude, enjoying an outdoor activity or pursuing a hobby. Whatever it is and wherever it is, a perfect day involves enjoyable activities and pleasant company. A perfect day is when you feel fulfilled and happy with how you spend your time.

If you were asked, "What does the perfect day look like to you?" would you be able to answer it?

Thousands of people were asked this question, and these are some of their responses.

There were a lot of responders that described their perfect day to be spent with family and loved ones. Being able to laugh and talk with them was something they loved to do; so simple, right? Some examples of these are "effortless conversation, lots of smiles and laughter, then not wanting to leave afterwards," "being with people that make you happy, laugh, and grow," "BBQ with friends and family, maybe a non-fire in the evening or swimming," "the perfect day for me is when I can spend time on the sea in my boat with my girlfriend," and "spending the morning at the park with my husband, exercising and playing." All these show that all it takes is the excellent company of those you care about to make the perfect day.

Others showed that people were finding that self-reflection and recognition from others would help them have the perfect day. Examples of these were, "the perfect day is when at the end of the day you get acknowledged for what you did and don't have to feel invisible," "A day in which I have the patience to deal with difficulties, the love to share with those who need it and deserve to be the best o can be," "at the seaside alone," "every day that I am healthy and well," and "being able to get out of bed without the heartache and depression with a true smile, not a fake one." When reading these words, you can feel some of the pain that shines through, but what is brighter is the strength they portray to face the day.

One of the responses that stood out was, "More often than not, we realize the perfect day after it's already happened. Can't manufacture it; it happens organically." This is such a profound statement. Being able to recognize that just because we can think up what we think our perfect day would be when it comes down to it, it's out of our hands. We can't control and plan everything, but we can remind ourselves not to take simple things for granted, as they can make a day perfect.

As you can see from all the different responses, everyone's idea of a perfect day varied. Some believed it to be spent with loved ones, while others thought being alone would equal this. Everyone will have different perspectives when it comes down to it; it doesn't make one better than the other, just unique to the person. If I were to ask you today, "What does a perfect day look like to you?" how would you respond to it?

- How would you spend your day?

- Where are you, and who are you with?

- Would you be working, playing or both?

- Find pictures that capture how you see this perfect day, or paint it if you're visual. If you want to be creative, use colours to show your mood for that day.

You might have too many things to fit into a day. As you reflect on this, you may be surprised how some simple little things make a day perfect; those are the things that naturally bring a smile to our faces. They are moments that we may choose to create repeatedly. It might something adventurous like exploring something or a place or peaceful like just having a relaxing day reading a book, taking a long bath or watching your favourite show.

Remember that we don't need to wait for a perfect day. There is no better time than now with what we have. Now let's think of a plan to start having more and more perfect colourful days coming up in your life.

Q37: How do you answer, "What do you want to be when you grow up?" Now that you are older

"When I was five years old, my mother always told me happiness was the key to life. When I went to school, they asked me what I wanted to be when I grew up. I wrote down 'happy.' They told me I didn't understand the assignment, and I told them they didn't understand life."

John Lennon

When we were younger, we all had that question asked at some point in our lives, what do you want to be when you grow up? We never always knew precisely what it was, we had ideas, and we knew what we liked, but as a child, there wasn't always a clear picture as to what it was. Or we might have naturally answered what our job will be or how rich we want to become, but how many of us ever said how we want to feel?

Many of us may think happiness or success comes with external things like a bigger house or a fancier car. Yes, it's great to have all that, but at the end of the day, how you feel inside matters for that long-lasting fulfilling life.

If you were asked, how do you answer, "What do you want to be when you grow up," now that you are older?" what would your answer be?

Out of thousands of people who asked this question, here are their answers.

One of the most given answers was happy. Many felt that they were at a place where it wouldn't be what they were to become but how they felt. Some examples of these were, "just want to be happy together with a good woman," "I think happy covers all aspects of our lives and continues as we grow older and age," "John Lennon said it best, 'happy,'" and "just happy and loved nothing else." These responders felt that if they were happy, then they had made it.

Some felt they would like to strive to become the best versions of themselves by learning and evolving. Examples of these were, "I want to be free, independent, and mature, "to be the best version of myself, keep striving at this and evolving with all the changes, challenges and experiences," and "from wounded to the healer, from consumer to creator and from enjoyer to provider." Each one spoke of how working on themselves, in turn, would make when they 'grew up' more enjoyable.

Meanwhile, others wrote about what they wanted to become or not changing what they already were. A few examples of these were, "full-time artist, not there yet", " I want to be an antiquarian, but I'm a nurse," and "more of the same, I am living life to its fullest and am happy. I just want to add someone to share our lives with", and "Definitely! If I look back at life, I won't change anything. Lessons learned made me who I am today. All difficulties overcome shaped my path." These individuals saw that their life journey brought them to where they are today, and those experiences made them who they are.

People come from all walks of life; as you can see from the responses, their experiences shaped who they are today.

Knowing who you want to be when you're younger, or even as an adult, is the first step to achieving your goal. After reading all the responses, how would you answer the "what do you want to be when you grow up question now that you are older?" what would your answer be?

- Now that you are older, whatever it is you are doing, are you happy?

- Write down or draw a picture of what it would take to feel that internal happiness beyond what you do for a living.

So many of us, when younger, are so eager to grow up, but once we get there, we wish we could slow it down to absorb every moment, learn, grow, and cherish the new experiences along the way. The version of success, happiness and freedom we may have had in our heads at different stages of our lives changes. We learn not to take the littlest things in life for granted; ultimately, how we feel about our self-worth matters, and that never comes with the shiny objects in our life, but it has to do with the light within us.

Q38: Would you go out with you?

"What you think you become. What you feel you attract. What you imagine you create."

Buddha

Many of us have an unrealistic approach to dating, feeling shocked when someone we are attracted to is not interested in us. Remember, our thoughts and feelings shape our lives, and we are what we attract. If we are happy with ourselves, we give that energy and vibe to the outside world, and if there are people we desire in our lives, we can develop those traits that attract us first. And if we are unhealed and wounded, we most likely attract the same. Everything starts with us.

If someone were to ask you this question, "Would you go out with you?" what would your response be?

Thousands of people responded to this question, and these are some of their answers.

The response that had an overwhelming number was yes; most would have no problem going out with themselves. Many said they wish they could find someone like themselves to date. Here are some examples of those answers, "100% I'd go out with myself. It's taking me many years to find my calling, and I'm 100% happy with myself", "Absolutely, I'm my own best friend," "Heck ya, every day," "Absolutely! I'm nowhere near perfect, but I know how to treat someone with the love and respect they deserve", "of course I would totally go out with myself and even marry me," and "definitely yes, I'm the best company I know." These are just some of the answers given; everyone would choose themselves every time.

There were also several no's; people could not see going out with themselves. Some examples of these were, "not now; I'm busy rebuilding my life. I need to fix myself first", "no, I would run," "definitely no, I think I would fight with me in a few minutes," "No because I need to be a better person, love me and take excellent care of me," "no, I find similar personalities very annoying, but my friends like that I'm a little different," and "no because I'm unattractive. People only like attractive people." So much pain and hurt shine through some of these answers, leaving one to think that their experiences make it hard to see past them.

Others said they had already gone out with themselves for a long time. A few examples of these are, "I always do!", "I always do; I don't go out with no one else. Too much drama, fakers, lying and backstabbing", and "I do all the time, sometimes specifically to be alone, with me." These individuals speak of how they are already going out with themselves quite frequently, and they love it.

As you read from all the responses, many said they would go out with themselves, listing why. But there was also a number that gave a big no, stating things like they weren't good enough, too annoying or weren't gay. After going over all these answers, if I were to ask you this question today, "Would you go out with you?" what would your answer be?

-   Do you like who you are?

- How would you describe yourself? What do you like about you the most?

- What version of you shows up when you are with someone you like?

- Grab your journal and list up to five characteristics.

When you come to terms with who you are or want to be, you'll have more realistic expectations of others and your relationships. So be alone, take yourself on dates, allow yourself to grow, learn what inspires you and curate your dreams and beliefs. By reflecting on your life and trying to understand and process your life events, you're giving yourself a chance to heal. You can show up as a better version of yourself when you are not carrying any hurt. If you desire certain things in others, you can be yourself first. You can only be sure of someone when you are sure of yourself first. That makes you more desirable, and I bet you'd respond, "You bet I would go out with me."

Q39: If you had one day to live, what would you do?

"Live every day as if it's your last, embracing each experience as if it's your first."

Jennifer Fertado

Living every day to its fullest is a goal we all strive to do. Being able to end the day knowing that we did our best helps us to feel accomplished and proud. A part of doing this is having those we care about be part of it, creating lasting memories, and living a life every day to the fullest. You've heard the phrase, 'live every day as your last.' It may be spending more time doing things with people you love. It would be whatever that automatically gives you a big smile even thinking about it.

If you were asked this question, "if you had one day to live, what would you do?" how would you answer it?

Thousands of people answered this question, and these are some of their responses.

Not surprisingly, most of the answers stated they would spend their last day with loved ones doing things together and making memories. Some examples of these were, "spend the day with my family and friends. Eat some really good food and lots of hugs", "spend it with my family with no drama," "hold a party with friends and family," "of course time with family, skydive, swim, ride a motorcycle, and talk with my daughter," "a beach day with my family and friends, have a big feed and just enjoy each other's company," and "spend it shopping with my daughter." Each of these shows their love for their family and the desire to spend every minute with them.

Others spoke of spending their last day alone, doing things independently and reflecting on their life. Examples of these were, "I would sit in my boat fishing with a beer until sunset," "go somewhere where I can be alone with my thoughts and myself, asking is it worth it or not," "drive in the mountains with my Cadillac and go skiing," "it's hard to say, I think I would spend the day somewhere in the mountains thinking that I worried a lot for nothing," "go to sleep so the time would pass quickly," and "go to the beach and swim in the sea." As you can see, there is a range of things people would choose to do alone, contemplating their life choices for the last day alive.

Another thing that had been repeatedly said was how they would not change a thing and would do exactly what they did now. A few examples of this were, "I wouldn't change anything; it's just an ordinary day. To everyone alive right now, this could be their last day", "the same thing I do every day," "nothing different from what I already do, I wouldn't want people to fuss," and "the same thing I do every day, spend time with my animals." They would choose not to do anything differently; perhaps that shows they are content with how they've lived.

I began by talking about how people strive to live each day to the fullest, creating memories with loved ones. I went on to show you the different responses given about what they would do on their last day and with who. They even showed you that a number would choose to do it alone. Everyone is different and how they decide to do it is what works best for them. If I were to ask you today, "If you had one day to live, what would you do?" what kind of answer would you be able to give?

- Think of the things and the people that bring you the most joy and ask yourself if you spend enough time with them.

- Write down, draw, or find a picture to keep in your journal as a reminder of things you may want to do more often that make you smile.

We often live busy lives on autopilot, waiting for the weekends or the holidays to do the things we love and spend quality time with those who matter most. There is some accumulation of little things that count that don't have to wait. Some of us realize this as we get older, and some, when a tragedy rocks their world before starting to appreciate moments.

Why not start living our lives like there is no tomorrow? Why can't we surround our loved ones and love what we do more often? Why do we have to wait for laughter for weekends and holidays only? I remember my dad always said, "live your life in a way that if they say tomorrow is your last day, you have no regrets," Do you live like that?

Q40: What is your best pickup line?

"Your talking to me? Well, I am the only one here."

Robert Di Nero

The truth is you don't need a pickup line. You only need a bit of confidence to say "hello." We can understand the behaviours that make us more attractive by being more self-aware. So, how do you do it? How do you become the kind of person others want to be around? How do you light up a room, even a little bit, and still hold onto the qualities that make you, YOU?

Take an inventory of your innate qualities like being funny, calm, intuitive, witty, a good listener, humble or whatever else it might be; it makes you believe in yourself and consider how to keep learning and growing.

If you were asked this question, "what is your best pickup line?" how would you answer that?

More than thousands of people answered this question, and these are some of the responses.

A number of those responding were quick to say they didn't have a pickup line or had never used one. Some examples of these were, "don't do pickup lines, all charm," "I've never used a pickup line, so don't have a favourite, should I start?", "I don't have one anymore, tired of rejection," "don't have one, always were too shy, not a confident guy with girls," and "I don't have a pickup line, I just walk by like they don't exist." It is clear from all these responses that these people don't feel they need a pickup line to start a conversation.

Others were the best selections of funny 'pickup lines.' Examples of these were, "excuse me, sweetheart, you just dropped something, I mean your crown, because you are a queen. I'm Alex", "I wish I had crossed eyes, then I could see two of you," "tell me, where do you keep your wings?", "you're so hot, every time I walk past you, I get a suntan," "I'm not a photographer, but I can picture us together," "are you wifi? Because I am feeling a connection", "they say Disneyland is the happiest place on earth, well obviously they have never stood next to you," "if Covid-19 doesn't take you out, can I?", and "quick can I borrow your phone? My mother told me to call her if I fall in love." People who use these lines are most likely the fun, easy type who likes to use humour to draw you in, which can say a lot about their personality.

Seeing some fun pick-up lines and some that would not say anything was interesting. What would be your reaction if I were to ask you today this question, "What is your best pick-up line?"?

- How do you appear when you meet someone for the first time? Are you smiling or timid? Do you make eye contact?

- List all your good qualities and revisit them often. They should be your affirmations to remind yourself of much you have to offer without trying too hard or being someone else.

Wouldn't it be fantastic if you showed up comfortably in your skin without overanalyzing it? Confidence is what makes you attractive. You don't have to try too hard or be out of character. You need to be more aware of what makes you drawn to someone; those qualities will also attract others to you.

Q41: If they made a movie of your life and played it for everyone, how does that make you feel about watching it?

"Life is a movie, and you are the star. Give it a happy ending."

Joan Rivers

Watching a movie of our own life on the screen can bring a mix of emotions and would be a powerful and thought-provoking experience. Movies allow us to think and reflect. They can even motivate us to live better lives. Let's remember you are the main character in your life, and you're filming your story right now. You can use that philosophy with the right mindset to tackle whatever scene. Becoming an observer of your life allows you to be more present and pay attention to the scenes affected by one decision, and you'll let the rest of the scenes go.

As you watch the movie of your life, notice whether there are more happy or sad moments, whether there are things you are proud of, moments that taught you something and how you would like the rest of it to play out.

If you were asked, "if they made a movie of your life and played it for everyone, how does that make you feel to watch it?" how would you answer it?

I asked thousands of people this question, and here are some of their responses.

A good amount of answers said that although they would be anxious or scared, they would also be proud because of how far they have come. Some examples of these were, "I would cry because of the illnesses, dark periods, and childhood trauma that I had to overcome. But the end would make me smile because of how strong I am", "excited and scared, a bit embarrassed. I guess I'm usually not the one getting the attention", and "Scared, anxious, and proud all at once. There is so much I have gone through, some unsaid. But I've come far, and that's the proud part." Although it would be hard, they would still be open to watching it with others because their story made them who they are today.

Some spoke of how hard it would be and that they didn't think they would be able to do it or would be worth it. A few examples of these were "sad, embarrassed, emotional, because I have always just survived, as a kid and now. Not lived.", "sad, because it's a sad story," and "I'd cry every time I watch it because of what I've been through nobody can imagine." You can hear the pain in their words and perhaps the healing journey they are on.

One that stood out was written in a way that showed both sides of the coin, the positive and the negative. "My life has been one of trial and error, success and failures, love and sacrifice. Family, respect, generational blessings, and enlightenment." This answer shows the growth and understanding of their journey. It also shows that they can see their strengths and accept their mistakes, knowing it's made them who they are.

Having a movie made about your life can be both exciting and daunting. After taking you through the answers, show you the different ways someone would react and their reasoning behind it. If I asked you this question today, "If they made a movie of your life and played it for everyone, how does that make you feel to watch it?" how would you respond to that?

- Are there any moments in which you are proud?

- Are there moments that taught you lessons?

- Would you adjust any scene, and how would you like the ending?

- Grab your journal and either draw or write your life story on one page. Trust the process, as it feels good to let it out.

It is a pretty emotional and powerful experience to watch your life story unfold on the screen right in front of you. The most important thing to remember is that we are the scriptwriter of our life. A good movie is unpredictable, just like your life. Tell yourself that your story is unique; it has ups and downs, making it exciting and interesting. It is called the different seasons of your life. You'd be surprised how motivating it can be when you believe you have a story to tell that no one has experienced. It is your unique life experiences that have made you, YOU.

Q42: What age do you feel right now and why?

"I am older than your age and younger than your body."

Santosh Kalwar

Each of us has a chronological age, the number we celebrate on our birthdays. Some, despite our age, feel more youthful, while others do not. Scientists can measure these differences by looking at age-related biomarkers like skin elasticity, blood pressure, lung capacity, etc. People with a healthy lifestyle, living conditions, and a fortunate genetic inheritance tend to score 'younger' on these assessments and are said to have a lower 'biological age.'

Aging is something that happens to all of us. However, we tend to view time as detrimental, always wanting to look younger than our age suggests. Your perspective dramatically influences how you view age; you can feel more youthful than the numbers indicate.

How would you answer if you were asked this question, "What age do you feel right now and why?"?

Thousands of people were asked this question, and these were some of their responses.

Most people who answered said they felt younger than their age, listing the reasons why. Here are some examples of those, "I'm 62.

Honestly, I feel around 35 because I'm a cyclist, and I'm doing 80,000-mile rides and feel great after I'm done", "I'm 42, and I don't feel like it at all. I feel like I'm in my 30's. Why? My soul says I'm in my 30's", "I can have the energy of a twenty-year-old, feel like I have the body of an eighty-year-old sometimes, and I'm an old soul," and "I feel like 35 because I'm very mobile and flexible. I'm 61." These individuals show a range of ages they feel, and one would believe that they are confident in how they feel and won't let anyone make them feel different.

Some said they felt older than they were; the younger they were, the older they felt. A few examples of these were, "I'm 28, but with responsibilities, it makes me think like in the 40's", "I'm 43, I feel older than I should. Constant stress from work as an executive makes me tired,", and " I'm 54 and feel 70 sometimes. After laying concrete for 40 years, I wonder why?" These respondents believed that their actions and life circumstances made them feel older.

Also, some said they didn't feel any different than their age, while others said that age is just a number. Examples of these were, "you're only as old as you feel," "40, because age is all in mind", "I feel the same as always, nothing has changed, I'm just older and wiser," and "what is age but an arrangement with time and effort." As you can tell from their answers, they focus on what lessons they have learned instead of thinking they had those lessons because of their age.

The range of answers that were given showed the different mindsets people had regarding their age. Everyone had their thoughts and examples of why they felt like they did. Some felt younger, others older, while some felt the same. If I were to ask you this question today, "What age do you feel right now and why?" how would you answer that?

- Do you care for yourself by paying attention to your diet, exercise, and mindfulness?

- Do you ever try doing new things by constantly learning and challenging yourself?

- Write down a list of things you must start doing to feel at your best, inside and out.

Simply asking people how old they feel and hearing them answer may tell you a lot about their health and well-being. Everyone experiences life differently. Our lifestyle choices affect us tremendously. Staying active, getting enough sleep, eating a healthy diet, cultivating meaningful and healthy relationships and trying new things can help us feel more energetic, vibrant and alive. Feeling youthful is a choice. It is not just our physical age but also our emotional and mental vitality that can stay with us throughout our life.

Q43: What have you learned from your mistakes?

"The only real mistake is the one from which we learn nothing."

Henry Ford

One of our biggest mistakes is assuming that we always learn from our mistakes. But have you? There is not a single person on this planet who has never made a mistake. Mistakes happen often, and if you learn from them, you often lower the chances of repeating the same one. But this is not always the case; sometimes, it takes several times to make the same mistake before we finally understand the lesson. Learning from our mistakes does not happen automatically, it requires thinking and reflection.

Mistakes are inevitable and can give us feedback and more creative ways of handling obstacles, help us develop resilience, avoid future mistakes and teach us humility, as we are not always right and can be wrong many times.

If you were asked, "What have you learned from your mistakes?" would you be able to answer it?

After asking thousands of people, these are some of their responses.

Most people said they learned from their mistakes, were able to get value from lessons and moved on. Some examples of these were, "Don't make emotional decisions, just logical ones. But also trust my intuition", "none have been so bad that I can't get over them," and "I learned to make lessons and to benefit from it in the future," "to trust my gut and don't be afraid to question things. Also, to use the experiences as steppingstones in my growth journey", and "when you need help, simply ask." The lessons these responses show are ones they could internalize and use in the future.

Other examples of this showed the mindset they developed after making a mistake and learning from it. Some of those were, "We will continue to make new mistakes, and that's ok; it's a part of living and growing," "it's ok to be human," and "very costly, I've made a few, therefore I've become a refined over-thinker, and that has saved me from lots of trouble," and "to proceed with caution." Each took a painful or difficult situation and turned it into a positive one.

While others didn't have positive outlooks, examples of these were, "don't give people things just to make them happy," "don't sacrifice anything for anyone! Just give enough and expect the worse", and "repeat them stupidly because all my mistakes are my falling in love again and again," and "trust no one when feelings are exposed, never give you all because at the end you'll be the one left to pick up the pieces." You can feel the heartache coming from the answers and hear the tone of despair.

One that stood out, that summed everything up perfectly was, "No one sets out to make bad decisions. Context and timing are drivers." There is so much truth to this. Who sets out every day thinking they want to make mistakes, not caring what the outcome will be? Tossing caution to the wind and behaving recklessly? Not many.

As you read through all the responses and the different experiences everyone had, there were lessons learned. If I were to ask you today, "What have you learned from your mistakes?" how would you answer that?

- Do you consciously continue to learn new things?

- Do you blame other people for your unhappiness?

- Do you use your time efficiently?

- Write down a list of lessons learned.

You are what you do every day. That means you can turn your life around today simply by doing something small that positively impacts your life. And what if you make mistakes? Just accept that mistakes will happen; it is part of life, and it is okay. It is important to approach mistakes with a growth mindsest and a willingness to learn from them. All we can do is open our minds to the journey, and that's how we learn and grow. Once we take responsibility for our actions, instead of blaming others, we can use the mistake as a growth opportunity and move on with our lives.

Q44: Not having to check off your decisions with anyone, does that make you feel free or lonely? Why?

"When nobody wakes you up in the morning and when nobody waits for you at night and when you can do whatever you want. What do you call it, freedom or loneliness?"

Charles Bukowski

Free or lonely? It's a matter of perspective. It depends on how you understand freedom. Absolute freedom, by that meaning, that you can do whatever you want within your capabilities and opportunities with no need to obtain permission or face consequences can be its own prison. When everything is permitted, nothing matters.

Loneliness can be a freedom or a prison, depending on whether one sees loneliness as a benefit or a tragedy. It is important to distinguish between healthy time alone, where you are being productive, creative, and reflective, versus negative time alone, where you are self-critical or feeling lonely.

If you were asked this, "Not having to check off your decisions with anyone, does that make you feel free or lonely? Why?" how would you answer it?

Thousands of people were asked this question, and here are some of their responses.

Although most of the answers were that they would feel free, a high number said they were lonely. Some felt that checking in with someone would motivate them, while others thought getting another perspective was good. Examples of these were, "lonely, brainstorming is a good process," "Sometimes lonely because I need someone to support me with whatever my decision is," "lonely because sometimes I need the help of someone who loves me," and "lonely because I want somebody to put as much thought into the decision as I did." As you can see by the responses, each one felt that having someone to check in with was a better solution for them.

Most did choose free for this question. Not having to worry about what someone else would say or try to change the decision was essential to them and represented freedom. Some examples of these were, "free because you don't have to share your decisions with anyone really and you're more in control since it affects your life," "it makes me feel free because if I take suggestions, they will destroy my plan so then I will feel unhappy," and "free because I have the freedom to decide on my own." Not having to check in with someone else made them feel free and independent.

Some responded with both, depending on the circumstances surrounding the decision. Here are a few examples of these, "both, free because it's my decision, but lonely too because you don't share the decision or can ask your partner for advice," "I think it depends on the decision you are making and the choice you have to make," and "both, depending on the decision, I'd say some I would like the option on of another, where others I am certain of what I want." As you can see with this answer, when it came down to it, it all depended on what decision was to be made.

Making decisions can be challenging; having someone to talk with may feel like you're not alone. But in the end, it's going to affect your life. As you could see from the responses, there was a range of those who fell under both.

If I were to ask you, "Not having to check off your decisions with anyone, does that make you feel free or lonely?" what would your answer be?

- Think of this scenario: You come home, sit down, and watch TV alone, and all around, there is silence. Is that loneliness or freedom? Some may find this absolute bliss and peaceful, and some crave company and connection.

- Now think of it this way: Do you need a conversation, a kind touch, energy in the room, someone who looks at you and listens to you as you speak about the things you love, someone to notice a change in your appearance, someone to ask you, 'how you are?'

- Bring out your journal and write down or draw a picture of your preferred scenario. Is it by yourself or with someone else who is there for you?

Freedom is sometimes where you find it. No matter how much you enjoy living alone, you may feel lonely occasionally. Having strong emotional bonds is the key to a happy and healthy life. Having solid and good quality relationships increases our life expectancy and give us more excellent immunity to disease. We are more likely to be doing well in other areas of life due to being supported and validated and generally happier.

Along with soul searching, living alone allows you to examine your relationships and note the ones that don't do much for your well-being. Having healthy support and companionship can do wonders while being alone can be better than being with someone that makes you feel lonely. Make sure you know when you feel lonely, do reach out for support.

Q45: What is happiness to you?

"Happiness is a state of mind. It's just according to the way you look at things."

Walt Disney

Being happy is a feeling that comes from having your needs met; it comes from within, with the satisfaction of knowing you are on the right track. Happiness is more than a good feeling. It's genuinely enjoying your life and wanting to make the best of it. Some people find happiness in external and materialistic things, while others find it in personal relationships and inner growth.

Happiness is a positive emotional state that gives us joy, contentment and satisfaction. Feeling positive emotions every day significantly affects our well-being, and that's why it's essential to do things we love and be around people who give us positive feelings.

If you were asked, "What is happiness to you?" how would you answer?

I asked thousands of people, and here are some of their responses.

An assortment of answers was given, and a lot had to do with someone else, making them happy or seeing them happy, which brought them joy. Some examples of these were "seeing my kid grow with a smile on his face," "happiness to me is seeing my family and friends happy," "the health and happiness of my daughter and a peacefulness in my life," "seeing my 83-year-old mom laugh at my jokes", and "happiness is me making other people smile and feel good about themselves." As you can see from the responses, being able to contribute to someone else's happiness is something that brings joy to their own lives. At the same time, others said that seeing someone else happy brought them contentment.

Others were based on their journey within and what they could achieve with growth and mindset. Examples of these were, "for me, happiness is living in harmony with myself and the world around me, inner peace," "it's an inner peace when you lay on your bed and say to yourself 'today was a good day, well done,'" "living in peace and harmony with your mind, body and soul," "health and balanced life that includes good challenges to grow from and of course some adventure," "living each day being the best authentic version of myself, healthy with peace and drama free "and "feeling good in my mind and body." For these individuals, being able to experience the feeling within helps them to radiate it to the world.

Many didn't know what happiness was or the last time they felt it. Here are a few of those responses, "to be honest, I don't know, it's a feeling I felt a very long time ago," "sorry, I can't remember," and "I can't answer that anymore." When you read these short but powerful answers, you can feel the pain behind them.

As you can see from all the responses, everyone's idea of what happiness means to them is different and depends on where you are at, at that given time. If I were to ask you this question today, "what is happiness to you?" how would you answer it?

- Think of how often you experience happiness in your life.

- What are some of the obstacles that prevent you from being happy?

- Write a list of things you can do to cultivate more happiness.

Happiness is a multidimensional experience that depends on many things including our genetics, environment, personality, value and choices we make in life. It is not realistic to expect to be happy all the time. The level of happiness varies based on our life events and circumstance.

Start your day with something that puts you in a good mood. It can be music, listening to a few minutes of a podcast, journaling your thoughts, and simply writing down positive affirmations about your wish for the day ahead. After doing these for a while, they become habits that fit into your day without you thinking about them often. That's when you move on to building a new daily practice. All the small actions add up to creating that feeling of happiness. Do one thing a day that brings joy to your life. It can be something small; it is anything that makes you smile.

Q46: How do you know your person is the one?

"Even after all this time, the sun never says to the earth 'you owe me,' look what happens with a love like that. It lights up the whole sky."

Hafez

Regardless of whether you're on board with the idea that there's just one single person out there, among the 8 billion people on Earth, that you spend the rest of your life with, the fact remains that some people are just better suited for each other than others. Theoretically, there can be many 'The Ones' throughout your life. We change and evolve, and so do other people.

But when you find "The One," you'll know. It is when you can be the most vulnerable version of yourself and still feel safe. You have similar values and goals, they root for you like no one else, you find a way to compromise and work through disagreement, and they bring you a sense of comfort and safety. You see a future together, and that makes you feel pure happiness. Finding your person is one of the most amazing feelings in the world.

If you were asked this, "How do you know your person is the one?" what would your answer be?

Out of thousands of people who asked this, here are some of their responses.

Many answered that it was a feeling instead of an action that led them to believe they had found the one in their person. Some examples of these are, "you have butterflies every time you see him," "it's a feeling of peace and belonging when you meet your soulmate. Both soulmates are connected through a higher power, it's destiny", "because of being in the moment and feeling it's love at first sight or feeling you would risk it all and don't doubt or fear the results," "when you know, you know, and there is no question about it," and "she feels right." Each response shows the emotional connection one feels when one knows they are the one for them.

There were also many answers where they spoke of actions that showed them this was their person. Examples of these were, "no matter how hard your struggle between the two of you, you still come back together with a pure heart," and "I know because she has guided me through many situations, I would have failed alone. She keeps me grounded and pointed towards God", "because every second of the day I think about her, and when I finally get to talk to her, I can't help but smile," and "they are always consistent with their actions. They love, value, and respect themselves and you." They say that actions speak louder than words, and to these respondents, that is the case.

The most significant response was, "13 years married, five children, three our own and two adopted, and still, my heart skips a beat every time I see my wife and enjoy every minute with her." This individual has gone through a lot with his person, marriage, kids, and adoption, and he still gets that feeling when he sees her as if his heart has dropped. From the tone of his words, you can tell that he can't imagine his life without her and that he feels she completes him.

Now that you have read the responses hear how people knew their person was the one. Felt the range of emotions that were shared as to why they believed them to be the one and saw the different actions that confirmed this for them. If I were to ask you right now, "How do you know your person is the one?" how would you answer?

- Do you have a solid physical and emotional connection?

- Do you share similar values and goals for your future?

- Do you feel comfortable being yourself with each other?

- Do you feel you can rely on each other and support each other's growth?

- Do you trust and respect each other?

- Do you see building a life with each other long term?

- List all the qualities that matter to you and make you feel like you are at home with them. Put a picture of them in your journal, or leave a space for it to come.

We are all impacted by our relationships. We must remember that no one is perfect, and relationships require compromise. When you meet your person and know they are the one, you feel a sense of home and can't imagine your life without them. If you are lucky enough to find your person, and even more so, know that they are the one, your life will be more prosperous as you can grow and be your true self in a safe environment. I bet nobody wants to live with pretense. We all desire complete acceptance, security, support and love that doesn't expire.

Q47: When was the last time you did something for the first time?

"The first time you do a thing is always exciting."

Agatha Christie

Trying something new for the first time can be exciting and fun but also nerve-racking. Every new thing we try is an opportunity for growth and new learning that can help us navigate our lives. Although there may be nerves that try to stop you initially, you feel proud of yourself when you can learn to push through them. Remember when we were young, so much of life was new; we often did things we'd never done. Don't you think it is important to recapture those feelings, especially when life starts feeling routine?

If you were asked, "When was the last time you did something for the first time?" how would you respond?

I asked thousands of people, and these were some of the answers.

Out of all the people that responded, a large number could not remember the last time they did something for the first time. They were unable to draw on one memory that displayed doing something new. Some examples of these were, "I don't remember," "I have no idea, a routine had become my life," "trying to figure out when I had," and "oh, I had to stop and think hard." None of these people could come up with one thing they tried for the first time. Why is that? What is stopping them?

Meanwhile, quite a few were able to answer, some stating every day they did or were able to pinpoint the last time. Examples of these were, "I'm sixty years old and had my hair coloured, foils, everything," "Last weekend, I went deer hunting for the first time," "five months ago I saw my baby being born, I was so scared of the blood, but I experienced every single moment," "currently every day. I'm starting a business and must learn quickly, attend courses and pass tests. It's both interesting and uncomfortable", and "yesterday, I made Vietnamese sweet and spicy sauce. First time and it was fantastic." Each one of these responses shows strength and determination, and it's apparent from the array of answers that they felt a sense of pride and joy by doing these things.

A few spoke of them trying something new, which is backfiring or causing pain and suffering. These examples were, "yesterday I decided to walk away from him. It hurts, but I feel free", "I opened myself to a woman. I was crushed, I still love her", and " last time I thought I did what I thought was something for the first time, but it wasn't and crushed me." You can hear the pain in these written words and feel the defeat with every letter.

Many could not recall the last time they did something for the first time, while others had some unique experiences when they did. You read all the examples and heard the excitement and some pain in the answers. If I were to ask you this question today, "When was the last time you did something for the first time?" what would your response be?

- Close your eyes and think of something you always wanted to do but never dared. It can be anything like writing a poem, a novel, or a drawing.

- Grab your journal and write or draw something for the first time.

Being able to try something new takes a lot of courage, especially if it's something out of your comfort zone. Taking that step and embracing the experience; will teach you many things about yourself that you may have never known until you tried. The scarier it is, the more significant its impact may be on you. But really, it doesn't have to be something crazy or big. It can be anything you never considered being open to experiencing before.

Next time you put off doing something for the first time because it might make you feel anxious, step back, take a deep breath, and then go for it. Think of it this way, if not now, then when? You never know; you might be surprised by what you'll come up with, and I promise anything you put love and passion into, the result might be something extraordinary that may even shock you.

Q48: What part of your life do you like the most? Why?

"My favourite part of life is when I laugh with people I love."

Dominic Welsh

Our life is like a blank canvas, a space we fill with whatever we choose. It is the story we tell ourselves every day. We can choose to dwell on the past and all the "What ifs" or make every day a new opportunity to grow, be better and do better. Many of us grow up with dreams of who we want to become, what to have and the person we want. As we chase the pursuit of happiness, to get the education we always wanted, our ideal job, the dream vacations, dream home or car and having a family, we sometimes forget to take a step back and look at every moment passing by. Remember, we can choose to live each moment consciously as they never return.

Our life is our choice; we can focus on all the positives and all we have instead of what we don't have or still need to have. Everyone's perspective is different depending on their upbringing. It can include freedom of belief, living your truth, travelling wherever you want, being healthy and happy, and having someone to rely on. It can also be things that we might often not even think about, like the resources we have access to, like having healthy food, clean water and air, hot shower, the food we eat, and much more which might be scarce in other parts of the world.

If you were asked, "What part of your life do you like the most? Why?" would you be able to answer it?

Thousands of people answered this question, and these are some of their responses.

Many of the answers given said that right here, right now, is the part of their life they like the most. Being present helps them to enjoy life to its fullest and genuinely appreciate it. Some examples of these were, "right now, because I am living my best life ever," "the part I am living now, going through a divorce, and I like it because it taught me a big lesson," and "right now, my kids are grown and gone, and my wife and I are having fun fulfilling our lives," "right here right now because there is no better place to be than the present," and "the present because I can change." These responses show their gratitude and love for living in the present and how fulfilling it is.

There were overwhelming responses about their family. The best part was being with their loved ones and sharing special moments. Examples of these were "my four awesome kids, two lovely grandchildren, and waking up every morning next to my soulmate" and "when I gave birth to my child. It was so fulfilling, beyond words, the love is so strong", "I love my daughter and being a dad because it's the one thing I know I'm good at. In all my failures, she is a win," and "my kids, they are the only good things that happened to me." The love was felt tenfold when you read these words and showed just how important their family is to them.

Then there were a few that spoke of a time in their life when they were stress-free. A few examples of these were, "riding my Harley along the beautiful Myrtle Beach, I feel so free with the wind running through my hair, and the only sound is my pipes," "freedom to be myself," and "when I'm singing, it feels like stress relief." Being able to find something that they enjoy and helps them to destress is something that allows them to face each day with a renewed sense of faith.

Sometimes having to choose one point in time that you think is the best time is not the most straightforward task, especially if you have many. If I were to ask you this question today, "What part of your life do you like the most? Why?" how would you answer this?

- Close your eyes and think of all your blessings, including all your resources and all the people you have in your life.

- Which part of your life gives you the most joy, or is it a combination of different things?

- Grab your journal and make three columns. List all the people in your life, including friends and family. List your resources, including all the environmental things that improve your life. List the things you love about yourself, including your health, mindset, knowledge, skills and personality.

As I started reflecting on this, I am very blessed and motivated to share my love for life to inspire others. I believe I have had two lives; a part of my life growing up in Iran, spending my childhood and teenage years in a country with so much restriction that we had no right to express our opinion freely, dress however we wanted, socialize or date whoever we wished or travel wherever we wanted.

Having all that in my adult years, as I spent the other half of my life in Canada, I appreciate the freedom to do whatever I dreamed. As I checked off many things on my list of living a good life, like getting my education, travelling the world, having a family, and living a healthy life, I gained more appreciation for the little things. The best part of life that brings true happiness is not your checklist; they are a series of moments making up what we call life, like getting a text from your daughter saying "I love you," Listening to my dad's poems, sharing laughter with close friends, and being able to help others.

Q49: Do you have any regrets? If so, what is it?

"Regret is useless in life. It's in the past. All we have is now"

Marlon Brando

When things go wrong, our minds may process and file them away under regret. They then can get pushed to the farthest parts of our memory, so we don't have to think about them. But why do we view regret as a negative thing, not a lesson? Sometimes the craziness of the day-to-day tasks gets in the way of progressing toward your ideal life. Time may fly by too fast; before you know it, you will reflect on your life with regrets. The best way to limit these regrets is by understanding what they might be and taking action before it's too late.

If you were asked this, "Do you have any regrets? If so, what is it?" what would your answer be?

After asking thousands of people this question, these are some of their responses.

Most people answered that they had regrets, some a lot of them. Looking back and believing they made the wrong choices that have affected the rest of their lives. Some examples of these are, "yes, some life choices, yet I wouldn't change them because I am who I am because of those choices and love where I am now," "I gave too much of myself to someone who didn't appreciate," "yes,

I would have told my parents, my kids, and most of all my wife how much their presence made in my life made me a better man," and "yes I do, I should have started with children at a younger age." You can hear and feel conflicting emotions in every one of these answers.

Some said they had none, choosing to see the action as a lesson. Examples of these are, "I am one of those lucky people who take adversity and bad luck to my advantage, so no regrets whatsoever," "none at all," and "I'm sure we all do, but the past cannot be changed, just learn from it and live smarter," "no because it's pointless" and "I don't dwell on any regrets, looking forward is what I focus on." Although they may have made some decisions they wish didn't, they have decided to be forward-focused and live in the present.

One response stood out: "I think regrets are better left in the past where they belong. Learn from it and live in the present." This is a profound statement. Reading this, you get an understanding of their mindset and the strength and confidence that comes with knowing that you aren't perfect and make mistakes, but you choose not to dwell on them or let them negatively impact your life. They are not saying that they never made bad choices, just that they decided to let the lessons guide them in the future.

As you can see from the responses, everyone looks at regrets differently. Some use them as lessons to fuel their behaviour in the future. At the same time, others use them to harbour resentment towards themselves, beating themselves up for making them begin with. If I was to ask you this question today, "Do you have any regrets? If so, what is it?" how would you answer it? Would it be easy or difficult?

- Think of a situation that caused you pain.

- Write a letter to show yourself love and compassion, listing what you forgive. When you get too hard on yourself, come back, and read this letter.

If you are unhappy with something in the past, try to make amends, acknowledge your regrets, show yourself some kindness by forgiving yourself, and clarify what you want to see in your life. Remind yourself that you are human, doing your best, and can only learn from past decisions and grow. Showing this compassion to yourself can help you accept and move past the regret.

Just remember, no one is perfect, and everyone makes mistakes. It's how you choose to deal with them that gives light on how your future will be. Lessons are there to be learned and not to create judgment, and once you understand that, it will be easier to see them as lessons and not regrets.

Q50: What are you glad you gave up?

"It is never too late to be who you might have been."

George Elliot

When you quit doing the things that are not serving you, you make more room for the things that make you happy. We develop habits that can either be positive or negative occurrences in our life. Sometimes they can spill into our relationships and shape them in a way that can damage us. The good thing about these is that they can be unlearned if you are willing to work on them.

John Dryden, the 17th-century English poet, once said, "We first make our habits, then our habits make us." Once an action becomes a habit, whether it's writing in your journal each morning, taking a walk at the same time every afternoon, or sleeping at a particular time, that's when change starts. Starting something new requires thinking more positively with a 'can do' attitude and a plan of action.

If you were asked this question, "what are you glad you gave up?" how would you respond?

Thousands of people were asked this question, and here are some of their answers.

One of the top responses that were given was giving up substances of any kind. Some examples of these were "drinking and smoking," "Smoking, it's been seven years now. Went from two packs a day to nothing", "3 packs a day cigarette addiction", "I'm glad I gave up drinking and drugs and wasting time decades ago," and "drugs, eight years clean." A sort of addiction took over these individuals, and when they realized that it was doing nothing but negative things in their life, they began the journey to stop it.

A lot also talked about leaving a toxic relationship, deciding that they had enough and wanting to move on. Examples of these were "ex-wife, and her brainwashed beliefs that held us hostage for years," "my connection to my husband, since he decided to leave me for another woman. I feel free", "my marriage, eight years," "toxic friends," "my wife of 26 years after her three affairs", "Staying in a toxic relationship that prevented me from leaving for a long time" and "my marriage has now been able to heal." The pain and pride could be felt through these words as they moved through some of the most challenging moments of their life.

Others were a mix of things stopping them from moving forward, so they changed it. These examples were "religion, an invisible man in the sky no longer controls me," "worrying about things I cannot fix," "working for someone else, now self-employed and so much happier," "trying to be something and someone I am not," "my loyalty because it caused me my toxicity," and "my attachment to loyalty when it's unhealthy." Sometimes what seems like an easy thing turns into a more significant issue, and until you get out of that situation, you may not realize what's going on.

When faced with a decision to change or remove something from your life, it's not always easy. Sometimes it takes years to realize what one wants and do something about it. Everyone is different, and how they approach them will be unique. Doesn't make either wrong, just different. If I were to ask you today, "What are you glad you gave up?" would you be able to respond to that?

- Is there a habit you have given up, and did you use a particular strategy that worked?

- Write down why you quit something and a list of what you gained from it. When you need a little reminder, come back, and review what you just wrote down.

Let's say you want to give up drinking too much pop because of the amount of sugar it has. It has made you gain weight, and you feel sluggish. You can avoid buying in the first place and replace them with flavoured soda water with zero calories. You are still drinking a beverage that tastes good and doesn't affect your health. And guess what? Next time you do your health check-up, your sugar level has gone down, you've lost weight, and you will feel lighter and more energetic. You see, changing a simple behaviour can make such a huge impact.

At some point, we all have something we don't think is serving a purpose to us anymore. We may not realize it now, but eventually, it will click, and you can start removing it from your life. Making changes is never easy, but once you start seeing the benefits, you'll see it's worth it.

Q51: Do you believe in the right person, wrong time? Why?

"The right person, the wrong time

The right script, the wrong line

The right poem, the wrong rhyme

And a piece of you

That was never mine."

K. Towne Jr

Have you ever found yourself in a 'right person, wrong time' situation? As the name suggests, this happens when you meet someone who could very well be your soul mate, but because of external circumstances, a relationship is unfeasible. We all hope to find a lifetime partner. Wouldn't it be amazing to have someone that adds to your life in all ways possible and encourages you to be the best version of yourself? Wouldn't you want to ensure that the right person stays in your life? But what if you meet them at a time when you cannot do anything about it?

If you were asked, "Do you believe in the right person, wrong time? Why?" what would your answer be?

Thousands of people responded to this question, and these are some of their responses.

The answers were divided into two responses. Some believed they could find the right person at the wrong time because sometimes life's circumstances can get in the way. Examples of these were, "yes, sometimes time and space collide just a little, and the timelines get a little bent with no time to fix it," "yes, sometimes the situation doesn't allow the romance to grow. You could be going off to school, joining the military, moving for a job, etc.", "yes because sometimes we are not healed so we can't receive the right person," "yes you feel and know that is the right person, but you also know that you are too late," and "Yes because love comes in unexpected ways." These responses show how they believe that being in the wrong place and at the wrong time could make the right person unavailable.

Many people believe this couldn't happen because if it's the right person, time will always accommodate. Some examples of these were, "no because the right person is always at the right time," "no because there is no wrong time for the right person because you will always change the time for the right person and vice versa," and "if they are right for you, it doesn't matter about the timing," "I don't because as long as we still breathe, there will never be a wrong time," "every person will come into your life at the right time with the right purpose," and "No everything happens for a lesson. How you react is the process, up or down, in growing the soul". As you can see, these individuals agree that if the right person has entered your life, it was meant to be and could never be at the wrong time.

Now that you have had a chance to go through all the responses. See the different views and opinions of all those who answered.

Felt the passion, determination and drive in the words that were written, and heard the pain in some of the words that were written. If I were to ask you this question today, "do you believe in the right person but at the wrong time? Why?" what would your answer be?

- Don't you think it is always the right time to meet 'the one,' so if you're unsure, you're probably not meant to be?

- If you're using the excuse 'the timing is wrong,' aren't you saying that the person isn't for you?

- Write down if you still believe in "The right person, wrong time?"

Remember, the word 'wrong' is there for a reason. It has nothing to do with you; you don't have to change yourself. Consider this instead; the right person is timeless. When you meet the right person, the timing doesn't matter. There is no wrong time to meet 'the one!'

While you should never completely give up on your previous life, the right person will outweigh anything else and makes you want to prioritize them and your relationship, no matter your situation. The right person will never stand in the way of anything in your life. They will encourage you to pursue your dreams and reach your goals. They'll lift you when you're feeling down and bring out the best version of yourself, and hopefully, if you ever meet this person, it is the right time.

Q52: Do you believe in second chances? Why?

"I did then what I knew how to do.

Now that I know better, I do better."

Maya Angelou

Some people believe in second chances, and some don't. The truth is nobody is perfect; we gain self-awareness through experience. If you change and grow with age, other people do too. Our personalities are not set in stone. People can learn from their mistakes; when you give them a new opportunity, you allow them to show their growth. Whether to grant a second chance depends on individual circumstances and personal values. Sometimes second chances can be beneficial; other times, they may not be the best decisions.

If you were asked this, "Do you believe in second chances? Why?" How would you answer?

I asked this question to thousands of people, and these are some of their responses.

Most of the answers that were given said that they would give second chances, some, however, did say they would, but it would depend on the circumstance. Some examples of these were, "Depends on the actual mistake and the motivation behind it. An honest mistake, yes. An unapologetic choice, no", "yes, because we are humans and make mistakes," "it so depends on the issue, if someone intentionally hurts me physically or emotionally, no. Thoughtless, then probably", "I believe in second chances because humans are self-correcting," and "yes, but you should make sure we learn from our mistakes." As you can see from these responses, if it were an honest mistake, they would have no problem giving it another chance.

There was a lot that said no; they would not give another chance no matter what occurred. Examples of these were, "no, because I believe no one changes," "no, you can't read the same book twice expecting different endings," "nope, not at all, you can't forgive, but you can't forget," "not really, after some mistakes it's never like before," "no, second time around would not feel the same. It would feel as if something were broken", and "never let an old flame burn you twice." Each of these responses shows that there was a lot of pain that was felt from the mistake. They thought that it was too much to be able to come back from, and even if they tried, it wouldn't be the same.

Mistakes happen, people apologize, and then they go on. But does apologizing make things better? You saw from the answers that were given the different thoughts on this. Heard the pain and turmoil in words. If I were to ask you this question today, "Do you believe in second chances? Why?" how would you answer that?

- Ask yourself these questions:

Have they accepted responsibility for their actions and grown? Can you forgive this person?

- Write down your boundaries and expectations to ensure you are on the same page.

We mature with age and our personality changes with our life experiences. If you consider giving someone a second chance, listen to your heart and let your intuition guide you. Ask your heart if this is safe for me. Generally, your brain will go through the logic and the ego loops, but your heart knows before you finish the question. A second chance doesn't often come, so if you are lucky enough to have a second chance, don't waste it.

Q53: Have you had a defining moment in your life that completely changed you?

"When a defining moment comes along,

you define the moment, or the moment defines you."

Kevin Costner

Our lives have many moments, some big, others not so much. But each moment has created who and what we are today. Identifying what they are and how they impact our lives can be rewarding. Some moments in life are defining or life-changing, including transitions such as immigration, getting married or separated, becoming a mother or father, milestones like graduation or retirement and negative ones like losing a loved one. They impact us forever and change everything around us for good. Most significant moments in our lives unfold naturally and spontaneously. We don't have control over all these moments, but we have control over how we respond and make out of it.

How would you answer if asked, "Have you had a defining moment in your life that completely changed you?"?

Thousands of people were asked this question, and these are some of their responses.

In every response, they said that they had had a defining moment. Several of the answers were just 'yes' with no explanation. However, many did have; these are some examples, "yes, becoming a dad and triple bypass surgery," "the moment I got diagnosed with MS," "I lost my job after workplace bullying. I stood up to them and then got pushed from my job, BP hit 220. It saved my life", "admitted to being an alcoholic and the actual desire and motivation to stop," "when I finally accepted who I was and came out to my family and friends," "the day I married and realized I made a promise not only to my wife but to God, to be the best husband and father possible in my life," "when my mother and father did not let me marry the girl I loved," and "my first trip to Europe, it was then I knew I belonged there." Such a range of events, emotions, pain, strength, and love. They took one of the most challenging and happiest moments of their lives and used it to set a tone for the rest of it.

Some heartbreaking answers tore at the heartstrings. Some of the most gut-wrenching experiences were shared. Some examples of these are "when my older daughter tried to take her life, not once but three times," "when my friend died suddenly and was taken from us abruptly," and "the death of my mom less than a year after my father's death," and "when my twenty-one-year-old got murdered nine years ago." Death will change us forever; when it is abrupt and violent, it can shake us to our very core. These individuals experienced one of the most devastating moments of losing a loved one.

As you read from the responses, there were so many life-changing events, some that people had control of and some that they didn't. If I were to ask you this question today, "Have you had a defining moment in your life that completely changed you?" what would your answer be?

- Think of a significant transition in your life.

- Reflect on an event that changed you forever.

- Write down how these life experiences made you who you are today.

A defining moment in your life can be either a happy one or a painful one. As Dalai Lama once said, 'Pain is inevitable, suffering is optional.' Sometimes it is a single event, and often there are several events. We all encounter ups and downs and learn from them all. They empower us, make us who we are, and change us forever.

As I reflected on my life, moving from Iran to Canada at 16 and sitting in first-year college, trying to comprehend a different language was not easy. Becoming a mother at 31 was the best moment of my life. Separating from my husband of 12 years and losing the only career I've known after 15 years at the beginning of the pandemic was hard. Getting published in a prominent Canadian Journal after my first master's and doing a global MBA later in life was exhilarating. You see, there were so many life-changing events. Some were up, and some were down, but they made me into the person I am today, and for that, I am grateful.

Q54: If you could travel anywhere, where would you go and why?

"I want to travel the world with an empty notebook."

K. Tolnoe

Travelling is a great way to experience different cultures and see the world beyond our backyard. Broadening your horizons can help you grow and evolve in ways you couldn't without experience. It takes us out of our comfort zone and inspires us to experience new things. It constantly challenges us to adapt and explore new surroundings, engage with different people, embrace adventures as they come, and share stories in the years to come.

If you were asked, "If you could travel anywhere, where would you go and why?" what would your answer be?

I asked thousands of people, and here are some of their responses.

Several people responded with places they would like to visit, some with meaning and others that interested them. Here are some examples of those, "Switzerland to go skating on ice," "Thailand, I was there before and loved it," "Guyana, because it was where I was born, and I love it.", "Makkah, where I can clean my soul and feel peace" "Arizona, it's so peaceful, amazing scenery, mountains, cactus, and sunset and sunrises, it's just priceless," "Scotland, so I can play St Andrew's Golf course, where the golf began," and "New Zealand, read so many books and just want to experience this country for a few months." Each place holds a special place in their hearts because it's somewhere they have been and loved, or they want to visit.

Quite a few responded not to a place they wanted to visit but to return to a period they wanted to experience again. Some examples of these were, "to go back in time so I never met the boy," "heaven, have a few loved ones there," and "back in time to when my mom was still alive, so I could see her one more time," "to go back to my childhood where I was happy," "to meet my dad. He was taken seven days before I was born", "to the day I was born so that I could find out who my biological mother is," and "to go back in time to see my dad once more, to say I am sorry." Out of anywhere in the world they could go, they would choose to go back in time to see a loved one.

I began this by talking about one's love to travel, the different experiences that they would have, and the memories they would make. You read the other reasons for the places they chose, the meanings behind them, and the ones that would decide to go back in time to see a loved one. If I were to ask you this question today, "If you could travel anywhere, where would you go and why?" what would your answer be?

- If you were to travel anywhere, would it be to a place or back in time? Why?

- Write, draw or find a picture for your journal of a place you'd like to travel and who you are with.

For those who love to travel, having the experience can enrich our lives and create memories. For those who think about travelling back in time, maybe it is a good reminder to cherish the moments we have now with those around us. Travelling to a place is an opportunity to learn, grow, remember what we already have, and appreciate them more.

Reflecting on my life, I had the fantastic opportunity to travel to many countries. People, food, culture, greetings, personalities and even the degree of happiness vary in different parts of the world. There are happy people in the smallest villages and the tiniest homes. I can always remember visiting a favela, the ruins in Brazil, with friends while doing a residency. We entered the little house, which was the size of my room with a woman and five kids, but it had a door, a window, a kitchen, and a bathroom which is not typical in a favela. She had tears in her eyes as she said in Portuguese how thankful she is to the NGO (Not profit organization) which has helped her with this home, and 'this is her dream home.' Dreams are all perspectives based on what we have and don't have, and there are moments like this when we are reminded of all that we sometimes take for granted.

If I had the opportunity and resources, I would travel to villages and underprivileged places, and there are lots of them in my hometown, Iran, to do anything I can to make a difference.

Q55: What is one thing that would make your life easier?

"Very little is needed to make a happy life;

it is all within yourself, in your way of thinking."

Marcus Aurelius

Have you ever considered making your life easier by feeling good? Living a healthy lifestyle is one of the most important things you can do for yourself. There are many ways to care for yourself by focusing on your physical and mental well-being because one affects the other. When you take care of your body, you have more energy, making you feel better mentally.

When we feel like we have an easier life, we feel happier, less overwhelmed, have a better outlook on life, experience more progress or growth and have fewer things that can take us away from doing things that matter.

If you were asked this, "What is one thing that would make your life easier?" how would you answer it?

Here are some of the responses from thousands of people that were asked this question.

A few of the answers spoke of tangible things that would make their life easier. Examples of these were, "right now, money would make my life easier," "winning the lottery," "a house," "financial stability so that I can finally move on," "wheelchair-accessible car for my son," and "free healthcare for all." As you can see, these all had to do with money; most said the answer was money. People associate money with stability; if you have peace, your life will be easier.

Many of the responses were about changes that would help and what they could work on within to make their lives easier. Some examples of these were "being the best version of myself," "not overthinking everything, my anxiety to stop and not to be afraid anymore," "consistent quality sleep," "being supported with love and kindness," "loving ourselves," "if my mind didn't overthink," "boundaries and accepting disappointment," "more patience with myself as I continue to grow and evolve," and "thinking less of the past and not overthinking everything." These respondents were very aware of what they needed to move past where they were in their life. Being able to work on themselves would help them create an easier life.

Unfortunately, many people didn't have a positive outlook, as they couldn't see that there were many options they could choose from that could start them on the path to a healthier mindset.

Making your life easier doesn't always mean going out and buying things or having a lot of money, yes, it can help, but in the end, it's not the things that will make your life easier. If I were to ask you this question today, "what is the one thing that would make your life easier?" how would you answer that?

- Are you paying enough attention to your mind, body and soul?

186

- Grab your journal and create three columns with these headings: physical, mental, and emotional health. Start a list of things you do under each category that makes you feel good. See which one you must work on and add to it over time.

We live in this world with a culture of getting everything we want easily and fast. Tons of fake wellness trends promise to make us feel better. Remember, anything that comes easy doesn't work long-term because it would just be like putting a band-aid on; once you tear it off, everything will still be there. The best thing you can do for yourself is to make an action plan that is doable for you, a plan you can sustain long-term. Think about a minor thing you can change and go from there by adding to it and remember there are health experts, depending on your goal, who can guide you along the way.

Q56: Is love a feeling or a choice?

"Close your eyes. Fall in love. Stay there"

Rumi

"I love you" are the three most powerful words. Love is the incredible emotion that gives us reasons to smile and teaches us to look at the brighter side of life. Love gives us hope and makes us more patient. It is one of the most beautiful emotions that makes our life worthwhile.

Love is making a daily choice, either to love or not. That's it. It is a series of choices based on many things, including chemistry, logic, where we are in our life, and what we want or need. We choose how we act in our relationships, how much we give, how much we show compassion and care, and how much of ourselves we share without expectations. It is the choice to stay.

If you were asked this question, "Is love a feeling or a choice?" how would you answer it?

Thousands of people were asked this, and these were some of their responses.

The responses to this question were close in numbers when it came to being either a feeling or a choice. Some examples of being a feeling are as follows, "it's a feeling because it comes without a choice like a thunderbolt," "feeling that doesn't feel like anything you ever know," "a feeling, something that happens, doesn't let other people's opinions interfere, follow your heart," "feeling from the bottom of the soul," and "love is feeling in love, never a choice, only for a player of love." These answers reflect how individuals feel like love is a feeling, not something we have control over.

Those who stated that love is a choice were very vocal about why. Here are some examples of this, "it's a choice to let your heart feel love again without pain in your soul," "love is a journey starting with a choice to reach a level of feelings," "definitely a choice, at the end you choose to open your heart to someone," "it's a choice, a commitment. Feelings fluctuate", and "it's a choice, I have not loved anyone for years now because I choose peace and happiness." Each one shows that they believe it's a choice because they think it's a conscious decision to allow yourself to love.

There was a higher number of responses, though; that said, it was both. The examples of these were, "it's both! You won't have a choice without having a feeling coming with it", "both, it's a choice to give it to someone else, and it's also a feeling," "you choose to love who you want to love at the same time you can't love someone if you don't feel," and "initially a feeling. Which turns into a choice in time." When you think about it, it does look like it would fall under both.

Now that you have read all the responses see the different angles from which one viewed love. I heard the tone of the words with the passion behind them and saw that not only was there a divide between feelings and a choice, but some also believed it to be both. How would you answer if I were to ask you this question today, "Is love a feeling or a choice?"?

- Have you ever chosen to love someone?

- List all your reasons for making this choice. When you disagree, revisit your list.

Although you may be unable to help your feelings and be attracted to someone, you can choose not to give in to your feelings. Love is more than a feeling; it is a commitment. To love each other is a choice we have to make daily. And genuine love is a series of choices. You choose to make someone you love their favourite meal, take care of them when they are sick, listen to them or be their crying shoulder when they are going through a tough time.

The choice to love is more than a feeling; it's an action. Love requires you to do something, and that's not exchanging flowers; it's putting your wants aside. Love is the commitment and time in effort rather than just saying those three words, "I love you." It is more like these seven words, "I got your back no matter what." Choosing to love creates opportunities to hit notes you can't hit alone, making your choice worth it. If you decide to love daily, love as hard as possible with all the cells in your body, and love with your soul.

Q57: If you could do something for a country, what would it be?

"Human beings are members of a whole, in the creation of one essence and soul. If one member is afflicted with pain, other members uneasy will remain. If you have no sympathy for human pain, the name of a human you cannot retain."

Saadi

We are proud of our country and may get behind it when needed; we might even fight for it and support it when we see injustice or see the suffering of others. Some have dual countries, the one where they were born and the other they've adopted, both call home. When you feel passion for your roots, it drives you to do anything regardless of the hurdles. Passion comes from deep love and pushes you through anything because you don't care what it takes.

If you were asked this question, "If you could do something for a country, what would it be?" how would you answer it?

After asking thousands of people, here are some of their responses.

An array of answers were across the board of what they would do. Some examples of these were, "improve its education and build houses," "get religion out of their politics and increase access to education for everyone," "change the human rights policy to be more accepting in all countries," "personally; freedom and equal rights for women," "protection from both foreign and domestic enemies," "eliminate corruption and equal justice to the rich and poor," and "spread awareness, and give them a voice, this is what they need right now." These answers show how they will help a country by empowering and supporting the vulnerable, helping them to be stronger and have a voice.

Two of the most liked replies show how supporting the youth serve the country better. The first is "Listen to youth and let them live, meaning let them experiment and experience life like others." The respondent felt that giving them a chance to live as they want, would help them grow with strength and confidence in how they live and approach life. The second most liked was "A governmental structure that would allow it to grow and serve those in the country." A government that helps the growth and development of its people is essential to most.

After going over all the replies, seeing the different views that everyone had and the ideas of what they would do for a country if I were to ask you today, "if you could do something for a country, what would it be?", how would you answer that?

- What is essential for you to have in your country?

- Write what inspires you to do something for a country and what it might be.

Sometimes our love for our roots drives us to do things naturally with no previous plans. It might be speaking, writing, painting, singing, or anything that comes to us naturally. I recently started raising awareness by talking about what is happening in Iran, where I grew up, on my personal Instagram, as all Iranians are fighting for freedom. It was like a wake-up call again after many years of blocked memories. This feeling of fight and flight of the child inside me has woken me up with anger and emotions overflowing, fighting back for all the years we didn't have a voice and being the voice of the voiceless.

Q58: What are you thankful for?

"Feeling gratitude and not expressing it is like wrapping a present and not giving it."

William Arthur Ward

There is so much to be thankful for in our lives, the good and the bad, because, without the difficult times, we might take the good times for granted. We might not appreciate love until we lose it, health until we get sick, freedom until we don't have it, and peace until there is chaos.

We got to remind ourselves of our blessings by practicing gratitude and saying or writing "Thank you" often for every little thing we have, so we don't forget. Mindfully practicing gratitude has many psychological and physiological benefits as it activates the brain chemicals that make us happy. It decreases negative emotions, increases empathy, and gives us higher self-esteem and inner strength, which ultimately helps us to have better health and stronger relationships.

If you were asked this question, "What are you thankful for?" how would you answer?

I asked thousands of people, and these are their responses.

The top answer that was given was their loved ones; they were the most thankful for them. Some examples of these were "for my wife and kids," "for my family, my friends, and my life," "for the people who show up and authentically add to my life," "life, faith, family, friends, pets, etc.", and "my teacher, mentors, and therapist." Each one has shown appreciation to those who show up in their life and show how much they care.

The second top answer was their health, being grateful for having good health in their life. Examples of these were "that I'm still wanting to fight for life quality, no matter how tired I am," "good health," "good health and a wonderful life, I am poor, but I am happy," "my health and the health of my wife and children," "for the gift of good health and being able to help those around me," and "clean and sober by God's grace." As you can see from the responses, they feel grateful and blessed to wake up every day in good health and mindset.

Others that were given showed a great degree of self-love. Those examples were "being who I am," "thankful I got divorced and love myself again," "I'm thankful for feeling enough," "for everything I have accomplished so far," and "of being out of my toxic relationship and restart my life again at 40", "I'm thankful that my mother gave birth to me because if she didn't I wouldn't have met the most beautiful woman in the world, my BFF Shauna," and "For my life and the chance to develop more kindness." These answers show that they have gone through experiences that have changed and shaped them and are thankful for the lessons learned.

As you have seen from all the responses, there is so much that one can be thankful for: a person, place, or thing, and even your state of mind. Each showed what was important and why they were grateful for it. If I were to ask you today, "What are you thankful for?" how would you respond to that?

- Write a letter to yourself and list all your blessings.

- List the emotions you feel associated with everything you just listed. Do you realize it is way more than you thought it would be?

- Keep adding to it whenever you are reminded of something new you are thankful for and revisit it when you are going through a hard time.

When you inventory all your blessings, you realize how much you have taken for granted. Every day we can find something to be thankful for, whether it's the roof over our heads, food on our table, the people we are surrounded by or who we have become. Not to mention many things we take for granted that people are dying to have in other parts of the world. It is the clean air to breathe, to dress how we like, walk on the streets without getting harassed, love whoever we like, choose whatever career we want, express our opinions freely, attend mixed parties, dance on the streets or sing whatever we want.

Being thankful for every little thing allows us to get through tough times, knowing that we are blessed with many things we often forget. It doesn't matter how small something is if you can wake up every morning and can name something to be thankful for. Start counting your blessings and see how much happier it makes you feel.

Q59: What do you wish you knew?

"If I am not good to myself, how can I expect anyone else to be good to me?"

Maya Angelou

Our life would have been very different if we could time travel and know all the secrets we learn with experience. Once we reflect on various occasions and consider mistakes, lessons learned and skills developed, we can respond more thoughtfully and honestly.

There are many things to list, including how others think, first impressions, friendships, relationships and being true to ourselves. Knowing it is ok to be different by pursuing our dreams, even if it doesn't fit the norm, and you won't know until you try. Lessons learned show us the limitations we didn't see before and can help us understand ourselves better. Once we can craft things that matter, it helps us realize what attributes to all of them. Does it all come down to our way of thinking and, ultimately, our mental wellness?

If you were asked, "What do you wish you knew?" how would you answer this?

Out of thousands of people asked, here are some of their responses.

A few of the responses spoke of what they wish they knew when it came to how they felt or what they did. Some examples of these were "how to keep an open mind, no matter what others do," "how to recover from depression," "I wish I knew about narcissistic personalities, I didn't know how common that was until after," "childhood traumas and how to heal," "how important self-love and boundaries are," "how to love without expecting the worse," and "I wish it knew earlier that we create our reality with our thoughts, feels, and beliefs." Through these answers, you can see how tormented they felt from their experiences, not knowing if how they reacted was the norm until much later. Wishing they could go back and give themselves this knowledge.

Other responses involved other people and what experiences they went through with them. Examples of these were, "that my father was a narcissist, I loved him so much I overlooked seeing who he was," "I wish I knew that some people can be toxic," "I wish I knew that there are people close to you, close family, who are toxic covered narcissist who will try to destroy your life," and "that my husband was going to leave me and throw me to the wolves." These individuals wish they could go back and know the signs that would help them not go through the pain they did, to recognize that it was never about them.

The most liked answer to this was, "I wish I knew earlier that not all people are trustworthy." In reading this of the respondent, you get the feeling that they have had a few experiences that have left them feeling like their trust has been broken over and over. If they had known this sooner, they would have been able to save themselves from a lot of heartaches.

You can see the desire to go back in time and change some things through the responses you read. If I were to ask you, "what do you wish you knew today?" how would you answer it?

- Reflect on your life experiences and think about areas you lack knowledge and skills.

- Write honestly and precisely what you wish you had known and why.

We learn life lessons through the consequences of our actions. Once we reflect on them gives us a lot of insight into how we think, act and react in certain situations. Hindsight truly is 20/20 because if we knew the outcome of our choices and their effects, we would have made a different choice. However, if you could redo a decision you made in the past, wouldn't that impact the person you are today? Changing what you did would also mean changing who you are right now. We are who we are because of everything we have gone through, and stronger as long as we learn from them all.

Q60: What is your #1 priority?

"If it's a priority, you'll find a way. If it isn't, you'll find an excuse."

Jim Rohn

Our priorities often change depending on where we are in our life and how we feel. Being able to prioritize what is important to us matters because of its impact on our lives and those around us. Our ability to move forward and accomplish our goals often depends on our priorities. Once you are clear on your priorities, you can make better decisions. As you start thinking about this, consider where you consider yourself on your priority list.

If you were asked this question, "What is your #1 priority?" would you be able to answer it?

Thousands of people answered this, and here are some of their responses.

The number one answer to this was 'myself.' They felt that making themselves their priority would have a rippling effect on the rest of their life. A few examples of these were, "to keep me healthy and happy so that I can be a good father to my daughter," "my wellbeing and peace of mind," and "my overall physical and mental health. If I don't have a handle on those, what good am I to anyone else?". As you can see, they felt that by making themselves their priority, they would also positively influence others in their life.

Other responses that were given involved others in their life. Some examples of these were, "my children's physical, emotional, and mental health, always," "my three daughters and my mental health," and "my kids, I know some people say we should put ourselves first, but my kids are an extension of me," "my children," "simple, to love and support my family," "settling the lives of those I love," and "my boys without a doubt." After reading these answers, you can see their love for their family and feel that putting them first was the right thing to do for them.

One answer that had the most likes was "Having peace in my life." A simple statement that has such a powerful meaning behind it. Finding peace, let alone having it, can be difficult for some because their lives have been chaotic, and they have never experienced peace. However, they now understand that having it in their lives is essential to their mental health and others around them. What good will they be to others if they can't find this?

You have read the many responses on this and the different scenarios of what worked for them, felt the emotions behind the words, and the importance of each. If I were to ask you this question today, "what is your #1 priority?" how would you answer it?

- Write down a list of self-care practices you already have, including exercise, what you eat regularly, relaxation techniques, staying connected with others, and so on.

- What would you add to your list?

- Update your list whenever you try something new that makes you feel good.

We have different priorities based on our circumstances, values and goals. But it is important to identify what matters the most.

Without health, our quality of life declines. Taking care of your health by putting your physical and mental well-being as your top priority positively impacts all aspects of your life.

Your first and foremost priority in life should be YOU, not in a selfish and self-centred manner, but with self-compassion and understanding. Prioritizing self-care means investing in activities and habits that nurture you mentally and physically.

Some may feel that putting themselves first is selfish because putting others, like their family, first is more important. We may grow up learning that putting others ahead of ourselves is not only the right thing to do but would show what type of person we are. But by not making ourselves our #1 priority, how can we be there for others in a healthy way and be present for them? Generally, our best self means taking control of our lives. Feeling well physically, mentally, and emotionally affects you and those around you.

Q61: What do you most admire in life?

"I don't admire how much a person has,

I admire what a person does with what they have,

and I think that defines you most."

Ariel Miranda

What people admire in life can vary greatly depending on their values, beliefs and experiences. But most of us may agree that we admire things that make lasting impressions. Despite what may seem, it is not the shiny objects or superficial things like glamorous cars, lovely holidays, pretty faces, or luxurious houses. As nice as they are, they are not things we admire.

We tend to respect qualities like resilience, kindness, perseverance, creativity and integrity. Some may be innate, and some come with our life experiences. Seeing how someone carries themselves and how it affects others may encourage us to have those qualities. Anything we do towards our self-development and growth is admirable.

How would you respond to it if you were asked, "What do you admire in life?"?

I asked thousands of people, and these are some of their answers.

Most of the answers spoke of a quality they admired in a person, what they do with it and how they present it. Some examples of these were "honesty," "resilience and commitment," "ability to express yourself," "a person staying positive and pushing forward regardless of their circumstances and struggles," and "I admire the quality in people who can stay calm regardless of all life's challenges," and "humility, understand as the ability to accept and love ourselves the way we are without pretense." Each of these responses gives insight into what is essential to the individual and could be something they strive for, so seeing it in someone else could give them hope that they, too, can achieve it.

Others wrote about more of a physical attribute to what they admire of another. Examples of these were "how our hearts keep beating unstoppable until the lord calls us," "watching lives evolve and those that are thankful for their lives, even though they might be poor in the eyes of the world," and "I admire those who know how to bring the best out of themselves and others," "health and peace," "people who are just who they are 100%", "people who advocate for the voiceless," "individuals that chase their dreams and take risks," and "love and freedom, the free will, loving, not hurting anyone or anything." Being able to touch people's lives in ways that help them to grow and evolve and showing that you believe them to be worth the time and effort, takes a particular person.

It doesn't matter how much you have in the world; it comes down to who you are. As you read from the responses, a great deal of what was admired was how they presented themselves and how that affected others. You could hear the admiration in the tone of the words. If I were to ask you this question today, "what do you most admire in life?" how would you answer it?

- Think of the values you admire in someone. Is there someone who inspires you with those values?

- List the values you already have and what you want to acquire.

Once you peel back the layers, we are all on this journey; we like to be happier and do better. Knowing your strengths and weaknesses and acknowledging what you have yet to learn shows self-awareness. It requires mindfulness and deep reflection on your thoughts, actions and interactions with others. Self-improvement is not what we go out of our way to do; it takes vulnerability to acknowledge something we need to improve. Being comfortable is easy; it is the discomfort that improves our self-worth, and that is admiring.

Q62: What does freedom look like to you?

"Freedom is the oxygen to the soul."

Moshe Dayan

Freedom can mean something different to different people. It generally refers to the ability to act, think or speak without due restrictions. Our values and cultural norms also shape our definition of freedom. Freedom can be as small as having your curfew extended or as big as survival for some little things like being unable to voice your opinion.

Freedom is when you live life in flow when there are no constraints, whether those would be physical, mental, or emotional. True freedom is having a choice and living your life on your terms and not by the limits of external factors. Living free is also living life in alignment with who you are. You can live free knowing that you control your thoughts, beliefs, and fears; you won't be trapped and become victims of the rules created for you or by you.

If you were asked this question, "What does freedom look like to you?" how would you answer that?

After asking thousands of people, here are some of their responses.

Most answers were about the freedom to be who and what you want to be. Some examples of these were "is to live in peace with myself and free to do anything I want," "when you do not feel any constraints, whether those be physical, mental or emotional ones," and "being able to live my truth and life as I want, without any repercussions or consequences," "when you don't have to explain anything to anyone, peace and harmony," and "free choice in every aspect of your personal life without fear." These individuals felt that freedom was living their life as they wanted with no fear of rejection, just living their best authentic lives.

Others equated freedom with worldly things, where they can see it, and it's tangible. Examples of these were "car, job, home and social connections that I can choose to engage with or ignore," "countryside, wildlife and being by the sea, or kayaking or fishing," "Freedom= Having all the material needs to sustain life," and "holiday in the Maldives." Each shows that they believed feeling free would mean having the means to do what they want.

Some believed that the freedom of their mind was the true definition of freedom. A few examples of these were "true consciousness," "to live in peace with myself," "happiness," "peace of mind," and "being true to myself and others." Working on one's mind and emotions so that it radiates from within and guides you through your days is the ultimate act of being free.

Knowing what freedom is to you is important because it could become your compass for where you will go in your life. As you can see from some of the responses, it means something different to everyone. Whatever is happening or has happened in your life will most likely be the direction you will need to take. If I were to ask you this question today, "What does freedom look like to you?" how would you answer this?

- What are the limits to your freedom? Are they external or internal factors?

- Consider how you can use your freedom to make a positive impact on others.

- Write down or even draw a picture of what it feels like to be free and how important it is to you.

What freedom looks to one person may not be the same as what it looks like to another, but it is a fundamental aspect of our existance that is worth striving for. You are free when you know your purpose and can live it consciously without any control. It is your purpose that gives you drive and stability and helps you to maintain your calm.

Sometimes, depending on your external circumstances, society may lead you astray from discovering who you are and being who you wish to be. Sometimes it is the minor things we take for granted as we are so busy constantly wanting or chasing more. Consider something basic that makes you feel free that you never thought about, and take a moment to acknowledge that.

Q63: What is a controversial opinion you have?

"Assumptions are made, and most assumptions are wrong."

Albert Einstien

Controversial opinions always spark debates. There will always be that one thing that will set everyone off; it could be something you believe in, like or feel. We often voice our opinions loud, even if it is something not agreeable to everyone when we are most passionate about something. It is important to approach them with an open mind, respect for others' opinions and a willingness to listen to different perspectives.

What would your answer be if you were asked this, "What is a controversial opinion you have?"?

Thousands of people responded, and here are some of their responses.

The answers to this were all over the board. There were no two alike, and they covered all areas of life. One of the examples was, "it's not what you don't know that gets you in trouble but what, it's what you know for sure that does." So instead of your lack of knowledge getting you in trouble, it's the opposite. But doesn't knowledge give you power? The argument would be whether it is better to remain ignorant and close your eyes on certain things.

Another was, "love is the result of a chemical reaction in the human body." Isn't it, though? Isn't falling in love like having no control over how we dive into the emotional bliss called love? But in reality, those feelings we connect to our hearts are chemicals and hormones flooding our brains.

"A single man should not marry a single mom and make him responsible for the kids who are not his." For any man who thinks like this, it would be interesting to know what they would think of the reverse scenario. Should a single woman consider marrying a single dad and caring for his kids who are not hers? Or is that just a double-standard way of thinking? You can see how this would create a hot debate.

Their most controversial answer was, "Men need to lead." Women historically get attracted to men who give them a sense of security and stability, and these are typically men who can lead. But we also now live in a world where many strong women are workplace leaders, which can create a debate on why and whether they want to lead in relationships. If we live in an equal world, should that even be a question of who should show in the relationship? Isn't it a partnership, and both people get to participate?

Any way you look at it, there will always be a difference of opinions between people. As you saw with some of the answers, there were some outlandish ones. If I were to ask you this question today, "What is a controversial opinion you have?" how would you answer it?

- Would get defensive if you hear someone's controversial opinion?

- Would you ever share your controversial opinion with others or keep it to yourself?

- Write down what you believe is correct, but others may disagree.

Controversial debates may cause disagreement or conflict. So when we find ourselves in one, it is important to remember everyone is allowed to have their point of view. Once you know they are just opinions, not necessarily facts all the time, you can react more peacefully next time and listen mindfully with respect.

Q64: What is the most important habit you think you can learn that would positively affect your life?

"Quality is not an act; it is a habit."

Aristotle

Doing things that positively affect our life is both fulfilling and satisfying. Seeing the results when we do this can motivate us to continue doing it. It doesn't matter how big or small it is; if it has a positive impact, that counts. Developing good habits is only helpful if you know what will likely deter them. When you want to start a good habit, start by planning and focusing on adding positive things versus taking away negative things, and you'll be more likely to form lasting good habits.

If you were asked this today, "What is the most important habit you think you can learn that would have the most positive effect on your life?" how would you answer this?

I had thousands of people answer this question, and these are some of the responses.

One of the many answers that were given was exercise and discipline. Being able to take on this regularly helped them positively. Some examples of these were "running," "the need to go to the gym and stick to it," "eating little to no carbs as possible, which changes how you perceive things around you," "self-discipline," "doing tai chi at 5 am every day and don't think during the practice", and "exercising my body and mind." As you can see from these responses, they believed that doing the exercise and having the discipline to do it regularly would positively affect their life.

Some talked about self-growth; by doing this, they could live healthier and more positive lifestyles. Examples of these were "How to put down boundaries and stick to them without feeling you're boring," "practicing positive complimenting strangers and yourself, as genuine as possible," "effective communication skills," "the art of completion, finish my projects," "taking one day at a time," "journaling regularly," and "how to remove toxic people from my life, even if it hurts." These individuals believed that by working on themselves, they would be able to have a happy and positive life.

Several examples of what can be done to grow toward our goals are given. You have read the different answers and heard the desire to want to change for the better. Listened to the willpower and determination in each one. If I were to ask you this question today, "What is the most important habit you think you can learn that would have the most positive effect on your life?" how would you answer that?

- Think of what matters to you, like your health, career, family, friends and relationships and list some habits that would affect every aspect of your life.

- Is there a common habit you see applying to all of them? Write down some steps you need to take to get better at it.

Learning to embrace the changes will help you to grow and evolve, making every day a good day. All it takes is a commitment to yourself and the willingness to work; the rest will fall into place. Positive thinking and mindfulness can help you maintain good habits by keeping a level head, boosting overall happiness, decreasing stress and anxiety, and improving your problem-solving ability and thinking strategically.

Q65: What would you tell a friend with the same struggles as you?

"You'll never find rainbows if you are looking down."

Charlie Choplin

We all have struggles, one way or another, at some point in our lives. Yet despite the prevalence of mental health struggles, there is still so much stigma around it. How you deal with it and who supports you will get you through it. Having a great friend who is not only there for you but understands what you're going through is one of the best things than can happen. Every day we ask each other questions like "how are you?" and "What's up?". We must pay more attention to how someone responds to find out how they are. Next time you casually how to ask someone how they are, really listen.

If you were asked, "what would you tell a friend with the same struggles as you?" how would you answer this?

Thousands of people were asked this question, and these are some of their responses.

Many respondents could speak of how they related and offered what worked for them. Some of the examples were, "I know it's hard to see the light when you're in a dark place, but remember it's only a bad moment or day, not a bad life," "no matter how bad the situation is, it will change. There is no permanent situation", "you're not alone, we'll get through this together," "have faith, this too shall pass, we'll have better days," and "you are strong enough to survive anything the world throws at you, if you ever need any help, I'm always here for you." Sometimes, knowing that someone else is there to help you ease the load can do a lot for someone struggling.

Others brought it to a more personal level to show their support. Here are a few of those examples, "Don't worry what other people think of you. If you can look in the mirror and love what you see and are happy, no one else's opinion matters", "be strong, it's about to carry the weight and improve your resilience," and "I know it's hard to let go of that broken heart, but you can't live in the past, embrace that heart and fix it." These individuals could connect with them, letting them know they understood what they were going through and what worked for them. Through these words, you can feel their connection with the person and want nothing more than to help them through to the other side.

Everyone deals with things differently; the harder it is, the more support may be needed to get through it. As you saw with the responses, so many people can relate and want to share what worked for them when they went through it. You could hear the pain but also the determination in the answers. If I were to ask you this question today, "what would you tell a friend with the same struggles as you?" how would you respond to it?

- Reflect on the things that have helped you during your struggles.

- Do you appreciate when someone downplays your struggles? Do you like it when someone vents with you, or do you appreciate it when someone listens?

216

- Grab your journal and write or draw the best thing someone can do for you or perhaps you for someone else when there is a struggle.

Struggles are going to happen for all of us. Sometimes people see asking for help as a sign of weakness, so you can comfort your friend struggling emotionally by listening to them and letting them know they are not alone. You can give them an example of when you or someone you know struggled and needed support. Make them see that reaching for help is the first step to feeling better.

Remember that our backgrounds, cultures and experiences can significantly impact how we view help-seeking. Thinking about why a friend might be reluctant can be important in deciding how to suggest they reach out for support. Hard times exist for everyone and are part of life, without them; we don't appreciate the good times, and they, too, will pass.

Q66: What's one thing that you are worried about and one reason you know you can handle it?

"99% of things you worry about never happen."

Ave Mateiu

Having worries is a part of human nature. The unknown can be scary, we can conjure up many scenarios that can stop us. When worry sneaks its way into our minds, we need to take a step back and evaluate it, determine if it's valid, and create a plan to work on it to clear it from our minds. Worrying for yourself, a loved one, or the world is normal. But sometimes, even small worries can manifest in your mind and become so big that they become hard to handle.

If you were asked this question, "what's one thing that you are worried about and one reason you know you can handle it?" what would your answer be?

Thousands of people were asked this, and here are some of their responses.

Several different answers were given from all different directions. One was, "If people I love, love me back. I have healed 95%, so I know I can handle it if they don't." The most basic and essential need is love.

Another was "falling into the dark abyss again, but knowing I have gone through it already and have the tools and support to know I will be ok no matter what." Believing that you are strong enough to get through whatever painful thing life throws at you is one of the most rewarding feelings. Having the insight to know that these dark times can happen and being prepared with the tools to get you through it is the best thing you can do for yourself.

This one is one that I think most can relate to, and it is, "Heartbreak, I can handle it because I've been there before." Everyone has experienced heartbreak of some kind, with friendships, love interests, and even with the death of a loved one. It can either make you stronger or bring you to your knees, rarely in between. How you choose to handle it will determine how it will affect you for a long time.

Lastly, "Finding my soulmate, knowing she is out somewhere." Many people spend their lives wondering, "Are soulmates real?". When you find yours, you'll know. The soulmate connection isn't temporary. It goes beyond the initial chemistry and "love at first sight." When you are past the honeymoon stage, you'll learn the answer to the question.

The many examples of the responses you read show the different types of worries there are out there, as well as the thought process of the individuals. Each one showed the strength and determination to live the best worry-free life possible. How would you answer if I asked you this question today, "What's one thing you are worried about and one reason you can handle it?"?

- Identify what is causing your worries and ask yourself they are valid.

- List some ways you can manage your worries. Is it some self-care practices, talking to other people or journaling your thoughts?

- Create a plan of action and update your list occasionally.

You know you will be fine when you acknowledge your worries and can express confidence in your ability to manage them through practical steps and positive actions. For example, if you are worried about your health, you can plan to get enough rest, eat healthily and exercise regularly.

When you worry daily about 'what ifs' and worst-case scenarios, you can't get anxious thoughts out of your head, interfering with your daily life. If you feel affected by a lot of worry and tension, there are steps you can take to turn off anxious thoughts. You can train your brain to stay calm and look at life from a more balanced, less fearful perspective. It always helps to have a plan of action. If you still struggle, remember it is ok to seek professional help.

Q67: If your life turns into a movie, what would you name it?

"Life is like a movie; write your ending."

Jim Henson

Who wouldn't love to see their name in lights and their life turned into a movie? Especially if you have lived a life full of trials and tribulations with many victories. Knowing that your life story could help someone going through something similar is one of the best feelings. Every scene exists for a reason. All the backgrounds come from the director, who determines the sequence of events from start to finish. That director is YOU. So, what happens when something goes wrong? What happens when an unexpected challenge appears? If you believe that your life isn't determined entirely by chance but at least partially through your choices, perhaps the unexpected challenges are there for you to grow.

We may consider a title that reflects our unique journey, our struggles and triumphs, or the lesson of our story. Some possible titles might be "Against all odds," "Finding my way," or "Understand U."

If you were asked this question, "If your life turns into a movie, what would you name it?" how would you answer it?

I asked thousands of people this, and here are some of their responses.

Sadly, there were a lot of unhappy answers with the title reflecting it. Some examples of these were "disappointments and betrayals," "waste of air on silverware," "hard way to heaven," "buried alive," "the woman of broken shards of pain," "a series of unfortunate events," and "never-ending disaster." You can feel the pain and suffering in their words. It is not rare to experience emotional outbursts when you feel exposed and expect more out of reality than what is seen in the movie. But remember, the movie isn't over yet and still playing.

While still able to hear the pain, others chose to turn the negative into a positive with their movie name. Here are some of the examples, "what doesn't kill you, makes you stronger," "survivor," "unconditional," "and she did it anyways," "always believe," and "there is light at the end of the tunnel." These words show that although they went through a lot, they still want to look on the bright side of life.

The most liked comment, as well as the only one that was repeated, was, "It's a wonderful life." These four words strung together, mean this person counts their blessings and focuses on the positive aspects of their life. Another reason for saying they have a good life also shows the hope for it to become their reality. Remember, words have power, and they become our reality.

Lastly, some responses referred to a song name they would name their movie. Examples of these were "if I could turn back time," "the long and winding road," and "what a feeling." What better way to describe your life and name the movie than using a classic song to the title to bring life to your life movie?

Lights, camera, action! You have read the responses of the different names they would call their movies, heard the meaning behind them and the strength it took to be open about what their title meant. If you were asked this question today, "if your life turns into a movie, what would you name it?" what would your answer be?

- By watching the movie of your life, are there scenes that make you smile?

- If something goes wrong in the movie of your life, where did that scene come from? Why did you put it there? What did you learn from it?

- Write down how you would go about choosing a name for the movie of your life.

We know that we grow through hardship, but we don't often purposely choose a difficulty or do we? Throughout our life, there are lots of ups and downs. It will not always be up; we can't let it stay down too long.

Depending on our experiences, the movie title may be obvious upfront and straightforward, and sometimes it will only make sense at the end of the movie or might even take some time to figure out. Ultimately, the title should capture the essence of our life story and leave a lasting impression on whoever is watching it; it could help them understand themselves better by provoking thoughts and taking them through their journey by watching ours.

Q68: What would you do if you knew you could not fail?

"What you think, you become

What you feel, you attract

What you imagine, you create."

Buddha

Fear of failure might often stop us from pursuing our goals and dreams. The opportunities are endless; if you choose to believe in the process. Now think of it this way, what if you fail? You still tried, and you lived how you wanted to. You never had to go on thinking, " What if I did that?" Do you know how many people never dare to do that? If you don't attempt something, you'll never have a chance at succeeding. That is 100% guaranteed. So, redefine what failure and success are to you, allow yourself to experience the process, set a goal and be prepared to make changes along the way.

Wouldn't be nice to approach life with more courage and optimism and use your talents and abilities to make a meaningful difference?

If you were asked this question, "What would you do if you knew you could not fail?" how would you answer that?

After asking thousands of people this question, these are some of their responses.

Many answers were about what they could do for others and themselves. Examples of these were, "after losing my mother to lung cancer, I would make everyone on earth stop smoking," "I would remove all barriers and walls that separate the people of the world," "eliminate homelessness, starvation, and poverty," "I would bring peace to the world," and "create world peace, cure cancer, investigate all our problems." These answers tell you that ensuring a healthier world that gives everyone peace of mind is very important to them.

Others spoke of things they could do, career-wise, that they would try if they knew they would not fail. Some examples of these were "pro golfer," "screenwriter," "professional athlete because they're treated like gods," and "would become the next United States President." All these are dreams of the individuals that they would want to be if failing wasn't an option.

Some spoke of how they work on themselves and make more money. Examples of these were, "Quit my job and make the same money working with my husband," "I would learn to like myself," and "I would take all the risks I never took." Being able to go and put themselves out there is a way; it seems they feel that they can gain strength and courage that they would end up carrying over to other parts of their life.

The possibilities are endless if you know that failure is not an option. Allowing yourself to try and do things you would never have thought to do because the fear of failure was so great that it always stopped you. If I were to ask you today, "What would you do if you knew you could not fail?" how would you answer this?

- Think of your skills and how you can expand your knowledge in meaningful and exciting areas.

- Grab your journal and either list or draw things you would do that make you proud.

Think about it: if you think of learning a new skill like a sport, writing, drawing or playing music, but you fear failing to be good at it, you'll never try. But what if you do it and you become good at it? What if you enjoy it so much that you think why I didn't start earlier?

By trying, you are learning, and all this learning will help you succeed. Great things happen when you try and learn, not with "what ifs." When you think like this and allow yourself to push your limits to achieve what you thought was unachievable, you will open the doors to many opportunities you may not have otherwise. Each time setting the bar higher will help build confidence and strength until it comes naturally to you to step outside your comfort zone and pursue opportunities that align with your values and goals.

Q69: If your actions had no consequences, what would you do?

"Life presents many choices, the choices we make determine our future."

Catherine Pulsifer

A world without consequences could create chaos and mayhem. Being able to do whatever you want and knowing you cannot get into trouble is both a blessing and a curse. When you live a conscious life, you consider consequences and accept responsibility for your actions. You don't do certain things because you know as thrilling as they might be, they might hurt you and others.

If you were asked this question, "If your actions had no consequences, what would you do?" how would you answer this?

After asking thousands of people, here are some of their responses.

Some answers said they wouldn't change anything and keep doing what they are doing now. Some examples of these were, "I wouldn't change anything because there might not be any consequences, but it would still affect one's conscience, and that's harder to live with," "keep doing what I'm doing peacefully," and "do it again, maybe it will work the second time." It wouldn't matter if there were consequences; they wouldn't change it because they felt their integrity would be compromised.

Others spoke of what it would be like to do something that could have otherwise proven dangerous. Examples of these are "jump from a plane, kiss the first girl I see, tell the boss to shove his job" and "Jump from the tallest building, if there are no consequences, wouldn't get hurt or die and can conquer my fear of heights once and for all."

The most likely and honest answer was, "Park in a handicap space, golf naked, call in sick every day, maybe take A 118 for a joyride and pee on the empire state building while singing it. It's the best day ever." This individual was brutally honest, and by his response, you would believe that he would do this and has given it much thought. Each of these things listed here is an extreme action that could very well affect you once done. While it's incredible that he could be so brutally straightforward and honest, the ideas he has given can prove to be much more challenging than the consequences you would receive.

After reading all the answers, you saw the different things people would do if there were no consequences. I heard the tones of fear, excitement, and apprehensiveness that each represented. If I were to ask you this question today, "If your actions had no consequences, what would you do?" how would you answer it? Could you give a response?

- Is there something you want to do that might have consequences or may affect others?

- Write down what it is and why you want to do it.

Dealing with the consequences of your actions means that first, you accept responsibility; by this, you agree that you may be wrong. Everything we choose to do affects us, those around us, our work, and our relationships. Taking the consequence out of the equation does not take out the reaction it would have on the individual.

When it comes down to it, you need to weigh the good and bad and then go from there. We play a part in every situation, and everything that happens in our lives is simply because of our choices. Instead of blaming it on chance or someone else, we got to remember that any consequence is because of an action we unconsciously take. With this knowledge, we can choose to do and be better, as it is all up to us.

Q70: If you could start a charity, what would it be for, and who would it benefit?

"Be the change you want to see in the world."

Gandhi

Giving back to our community is important to so many of us. When you can make a difference with something close to your heart, it makes it more special. Being able to step up and help others is rewarding and satisfying because you are creating a future of hope and happiness.

If you were asked this question, "If you could start a charity, what would it be for, and who would benefit?" what would your answer be?

Thousands of people were asked this question, and here are some of their responses.

The most liked comment was, "A charity for youth at risk of mental health and homelessness called 'youth in motion '; it's something I thought of and dreamed of for a while now." So many people agreed with this, believing to help and prepare the youth for their future and allowing them to grow and evolve will do. Especially if the youth come from a home that couldn't show them support, having this would help them to create a healthier and more productive future.

One of the most given answers was about children, whether with their education, feeding them or teaching them a trade. Some examples of these were "would be related to sick kids who can't afford medical care," "charity fighting child cancer," "food to eat for children in a third world country," and "orphans, for them to go on trips and enjoy a fun life," and "ending child hunger and increased access to education. No child should live with hunger and education is key to a better future". Each one of these maps out the needs of the children and what can be done to ensure they have a better future. In helping them, we will also be helping our future.

A few others that were given were "pregnant women without any support at all, benefits the mom and the babies to keep them safe," "DV victims who are men, including a shelter," and "addiction and recovery for free to those who need it." These individuals desire to help those who deal with the less talked about because of the shame, fear, and stigma around it.

There are many charities, pretty much whatever you can think of. As you read the response, you could see the passion behind the answers and the need to help those who can't help themselves. What would your reaction be if I were to ask you, "If you could start a charity, what would it be for, and who would benefit?" what would your response be?

- What gets you out of bed in the morning?

- Who would you like to help and why?

- Write or draw a picture of a charity that you could start today.

When I looked within, I thought I would start a charity that empowers girls and women, a ladies club from all walks of life. The mission is a community of like-minded ladies who don't dare to stop growing. The goal is to inspire my generation and my daughter's generation to live happy and healthy lives. If you are a lady reading this and this sounds interesting to you, join the club, as you know where to find me.

Q71: What makes you smile?

"Whatever happens, just keep smiling and lose yourself in love."

Rumi

Many of us smile when we experience something that brings us joy and happiness. There is no denying the feel-good power of smiling. It doesn't take much to smile; it could be spending time with a loved one, receiving a compliment, watching a funny video, enjoying a delicious meal, achieving a goal or simply being outside nature.

Smiling is mood-boosting and affects our bodies as well as our mind. When you smile, your brain releases happy hormones, which help lower anxiety and strengthen immunity. Not to mention, people who smile are more likable, making it easier to connect with others. It can also be contagious as it makes others around have more smiles.

How would you answer this if asked, "What makes you smile?"?

Out of the thousands of people who responded, here are some of their answers.

Most of the responses spoke of how others make them smile, family, friends and even a stranger. Some examples of these were "Animals. and happy people", "When I get home from work my puppy runs to greet me no matter what he was doing before. my best friend", "children laughing," "my wife and children, every day," "seeing people I love, family, friends," "grandkids," and "children, animals and nice people." Experiencing the sheer joy of someone you love and care about is one of the quickest ways to bring a smile to their face.

Other responses shared how doing something nice for someone, even the most minor things, and seeing how much the other appreciated it was enough to have them smiling. Examples of these were "when I do something for someone else and see that it makes them feel good," "helping others along the road we call life," and "when I do something small for someone, and they think it's incredible." Being in a place where it brings you joy to do something for others attests to their mindset.

Some also spoke of different things they did that brought them so much joy they couldn't help but smile. These examples were "watching my dogs play," "Sun in the morning, air after the gentle rain and peaceful thoughts," "a good forest walk," and "Just knowing that I'm alive to see a new day and other people who exhibit positive energy through their smile." These individuals were able to find something to make them smile, choosing to see the positive to make their days a little better.

Smiles are free and make us feel good. Finding things that help you smile more benefits your mind and body. How would you answer if I were to ask you this question today, "what makes you smile?"?

- Let's try a smile challenge. Grab your journal and write down at least five people, places or things that make you smile. Look at them every time you are not in a good mood.

- Create a smile collage of pictures of you smiling by yourself, smiling with someone else or an activity or place that makes you smile. Post it in your journal or, if you choose to post on social media and invite others to do the same, tag me too to make smile **@hediehsafiyari**

The things that make people smile can vary greatly depending on their individual experiences, preferences and circumstances. Finding joy in the little things that make us smile is beautiful and rewarding. Knowing you can do the same for another person is also great. It doesn't matter how bad of a day you may have; if you can make someone else smile, your day will be much better. And how do you smile if you are not feeling it? You fake it till you make it because your body language can influence your emotions. If you are smiling on purpose to help your mood, smile until your cheeks lift and smile as you mean it. I hope you have a big smile right now as you read this.

Q72: If you could plan a date with your inner child, what would you do or where would you go?

"I am happy to report that my inner child is still ageless."

James Broughton

Your inner child is a part of your subconscious that holds memories, emotions, and beliefs. Being able to connect and nurture your inner child helps you to heal and grow. It encompasses the parts of our psyche that retain the qualities we all possessed as children, like the joyful energies of creativity, curiosity, playfulness, and spontaneity.

The inner child also describes parts of us that are wounded. Various incidents in our childhood, especially highly charged ones, may have left us with some unresolved feelings. We did not have the cognition to understand what was happening then, and often there was no one to explain it to us. These early experiences leave 'markers' in our body, mind, and spirit that show up in adulthood.

If you were asked this question, "If you could plan a date with your inner child, what would you do or where would you go?" how would you answer this?

Thousands of people answered, and here are some of their responses.

Most of those who answered spoke of fun things they would do with their inner child as a date. Some examples of these were, "go to the park with him and have the fun he never had," "ice cream parlour, carnival, toy store," "Disneyland for sure, play, eat, and talk about everything all day long," "baseball game where we can have fun, but still talk as well," "go for a walk in nature and then play video games," and "go karting, gaming, and finish it off with a walk on the beach." Each of these answers catered to having fun and connecting with their inner child in ways they never did before.

Others included ones that involved other people being with them. These are some examples, "supporting the homeless at a shelter with food, water, and clothing," "to visit mom and show her true great outdoors," "jumping with my friends from kindergarten," "having dinner with my parents," and "back to my high school era and create the fun we never had." Recreating a memory, making it more positive, can help with our healing and growth.

A couple stood out, showing the depth in which they would want to have the peace they believed they deserved. They were "watching the sea; I would hug her all the time telling her the things that will give her enough confidence and power to believe in herself," and "hug her so tight and tell her everything is going to be ok, she's strong, beautiful, and worthy." Everyone wants to be told it will be ok, even if it means you are saying it to your younger self.

As you saw with the responses, there were many ways they would spend with their inner child. Some spoke of alone time with them to reconnect, while others wanted to share it with others they loved and cared about. If I were to ask you this right now, "if you could plan a date with your inner child, what would you do or where would you go?" what would your response be?

-   Let's do this powerful exercise for connecting with your inner child. Close your eyes, travel back in time and think of five simple things that made you happy, like playing hide and seek with the kids in the street, playing in the waves, running in the woods and the smell of your favourite meal.

-   Remember all the senses that bring back memories like freshly cut lawns and warm summer days of swimming, building a nest for the birds, watching your favourite cartoon on the only channel, and cramming a big cheesy pizza.

-   Open your eyes and allow yourself to feel all that. Now grab your journal, draw a picture of what was going in your mind or write a letter to your inner child.

The journey you take with your inner child can bring you happiness and pain, depending on where you are at that moment. Healing can be challenging because there could be old wounds that have not been addressed yet. But it can also be rewarding because you would be helping them to grow and heal, and you would be helping yourself. Having said all this, depending on childhood experiences, some people might need further support or to see a therapist to work through some unresolved experiences.

Q73: If you could relive one day of your life, what day would that be?

"Be happy for this moment. This moment is your life."

Omar Khayyam

Living a great life is living in the present moment, letting go of the past, and not waiting for the future. There are many memories that we might reflect on from time to time. We all have had moments and people that we always cherish. A mindful life is living in the present moment. But if you could relive a moment, let it be the happiest time of your life. The moment that you never forget that your eyes still light up and put the biggest smile on your face. Do you have moments like that?

If you were asked, "If you could relive one day of your life, what day would that be?" how would you answer it?

Thousands of people responded, and here are some of their answers.

So many of the responses spoke of a painful time in their life that they wish they could go back and redo. Some of the examples were, "all days before my girlfriend dies, any one of them. 44 years now and still in my heart", "the last day I spent with my late son," "I would love to spend one more day with my friend who passed away this year, one more conversation, one more smile," "the day my mother passed away, as I never got a chance to say goodbye," and "the day before my gramma's death so I can call her and go hand out with her and tell her I love her." You could feel the pain and regret when you read these words.

Others spoke of happier times that they would love to redo to recapture their feelings. Examples of these were "the day my second born son was born," "the day I met my husband," "the days when I sat on the rock at the Pacific Ocean close to Carmel-by-the-sea, watching the waves," "having fun with my father when I was little," and "my youngest brother's wedding day." Such beautiful memories were given here; the love they had and the joy they felt is something they wish they could package up in a bottle and carry with them forever.

As you read all the responses, some would want to return a time they lost, even though it hurts a lot. But others preferred to be able to go back to a happier time. If you were asked this question today, "if you could relive one day of your life, what day would that be?" would you have a response for that?

- Reflect on the emotions you had on the day you want to relive and consider the impact of reviewing it on your present and future.

- Write or draw a picture of a moment in time that you cherish.

The decision to relive a day would be very personal and depend on each individual's experiences. Not that living in the past is a good idea; it is not. Because the reality is right now, is all we have. But if we had to time travel, let's think of all the good memories. You don't want to relive difficult or negative days. As I reflected on this thought, the day I would relive it again was when I became a mom and met my daughter for the first time. She had too much long spiky hair with big cheeks for a newborn; she cried so much, but it was the cutest thing I have ever seen with little fingers wrapped around mine; that moment still brings a big smile to my face as I write this. It was the moment I understood what unconditional love is.

Q74: What is the silliest thing you are passionate about?

"A life without passion is not living; it's merely existing."

Leo Buscaglia

Having a passion you can shape and mould however you desire is fantastic and satisfying. The crazier the passion, the more fun it is. Remember when you were a kid? You were led merely by your curiosity and excitement to play and explore. Nobody told you to do it; you just did it. Could you be that child again to rediscover your passion? Something that comes to you naturally. A passion, silly or not, is a great release and creates beautiful memories. Sometimes it can be tangible, or it can be something you do for yourself or others. Whatever it may be, having it gives you purpose in life.

If you were asked this question, "what is the silliest thing you are passionate about?" how would you answer it?

I asked thousands of people, and here are some of their responses.

There was so much variety in the answers, some light, others heartfelt. Here are some examples: "my global rock collection," "plants," "looking at the full moon, and let the thoughts glow by," "sports cars, especially from the 1960s & 1970's", "laying on the couch just chilling," and "music." While reading these, you can feel the nostalgic emotions radiating from them and hear the joy of doing something that brings them peace of mind.

Other examples involved something they were doing that made them happy. These are "stopping people in the streets and saying how great they look, or what they are wearing," "my alone time to stay away from people, so refreshing," "a peaceful walk with the one you love, followed by a romantic evening," "helping other people makes me happy," "working with animals," and "watching a movie with someone I love." Sometimes all it takes is doing and being with someone they care about to feel content with life.

A few people said they could not find anything they are passionate about, nothing that brings them joy or a sense of purpose. Why is that? What makes it so difficult to answer?

As you saw from the answers, there are so many things that you can be passionate about. You can hear the excitement and joy that was felt through the words. No two answers were the same, but the feelings you got from reading them were alike. If I were to ask you this question today, "What is the silliest thing you are passionate about?" how would you answer it?

- Let's do this exercise to discover your passion:

Make three lists. A list of the things you are good at on one of them. Next, write a list you enjoy doing in your spare time. On the third, write a list of things that gives you purpose. Is there something that you keep repeating?

- Grab your journal and write or draw a picture of something that is your true passion and purpose.

As I reflected on this, I was the kid who always volunteered to be the lead actress in every school theatre, retold the entire movie I watched with my parents the night before to my friends in school the next day, wrote little romantic novels and talked the most out of all my friends. Here is the moment I'd like to apologize to all my friends who are reading this right now if I talked your ears off. I was the storyteller, and that is my passion today.

Q75: What life event or experience changed you?

"Let nothing dim the light that shines from within."

Maya Angelou

We often go through something that will change our course, whether good or bad. It can be such a defining moment that we won't be the same when we come out on the other side. Personal experience leads to lessons learned. Consider all the things that have created significant changes in your life. Now think about it, has something occurred in your life that made you realize there was no turning back? Perhaps something happened, and you wanted to duck and take cover, but instead, you chose to face it head-on. There must have been a lot of learning in it. No matter how difficult something may be, you can always get something positive out of it.

If you were asked this question, "what life event or experience changed you?" how would you answer it?

I asked this question to thousands of people, and here are some of their responses.

An overwhelming number of responses spoke of something excruciating that changed them. Some examples of these are "when my mother died unexpectedly 13 years ago", "being pushed from a job for bullying," "my dad and little sister dying within six months of each other," "going through a divorce after fifteen years of marriage," and "loss of my firstborn." So much pain and heartbreak are felt through these words. You can feel the struggle in some of these responses.

Other examples showed some happy and inspiring moments that changed them. These examples are "meeting my wife and also a trip to West Africa," "graduated from university with an electrical engineering degree," "overseas trip for a year," "when I met my true love," and "studying the bible and meeting Jesus in those pages." Sharing uplifting experiences, knowing you are constantly evolving, and sharing this with others is enough to motivate anyone.

One response caught my eye: "change is the only constant in our universe and is non-stop." How true and profound is this? Realizing that change will happen, no matter what gives you a different perspective on life and how you live each day. Accepting this, how you view change will help you learn and grow, aiming always to live your best life.

After reading all the responses, although several spoke of painful experiences, you could also hear a hopeful undertone. Many said happy times they went through that were life-changing. If I were to ask you this today, "what life event or experience changed you?" how would you answer it?

- Remember a life-changing event in your childhood.

- Reflect on a life-changing event in your adulthood.

- If you could rewrite your life story, would you rewrite any part of it?

As I went through this exercise myself, got reminded that there were so many seasons in my life with significant changes. I went through war for eight years as a child having classrooms in underground shelters, immigration as a teenager where I had to adjust to a new culture and language, motherhood as an adult, and so much more. My life experiences changed me forever, turned me into the person I am today and made me more resilient. They taught me that I could bounce back from anything.

About the Author

Hedieh is a mother, an entrepreneur, a business consultant, a public speaker, and the founder of PromptHealth, a wellness app. She worked as a clinician for almost 20 years and created an app to empower those seeking wellness solutions and wellness businesses. She holds a master's degree in Cardiac rehab as well as MBA.

As a digital creator, she's inspiring thousands of people every day.

Want to know more about who she is? Follow her latest at **www.hediehsafiyari.com**
Want to know more about PromptHealth?
Visit **www.prompthealth.ca**

@hediehsafiyari

More resources?

If you are interested in leveling up your life in different areas, personally or professionally, Hedieh has created some additional resources at **www.hediehsafiyari.com**

Lifestyle Mastery
A guide for anyone interested to learn some basic tips to improve physical, mental and emotional health.

Mindset Mastery
A guide for aspiring entreprenurs who need mindset motivation and tips on building a strong presence.

Learn It Yourself
One-time package to access a library of videos on tips and strategies to boost your health and wellness business online.

ONE TIME 100% DISCOUNT CODE
FOR LIFESTYLE MASTERY

CODE: LIFESTYLE

Printed in Great Britain
by Amazon

23823752R00145